W9-ACR-559

The Trial of Joan of Arc

by Don Nardo

FAMOUS
TRIALS

Lucent Books, San Diego, CA

Other books in the Famous Trials series:

The Boston Massacre
Brown v. Board of Education
The Dred Scott Decision
The Nuremberg Trials

The O.J. Simpson Trial
The Salem Witch Trials
The Scopes Trial
The Trial of Socrates

Library of Congress Cataloging-in-Publication Data

Nardo, Don, 1947–
The trial of Joan of Arc / by Don Nardo.
   p. cm. — (Famous trials series)
   Includes bibliographical references and index.
   Summary: Describes the 1431 trial of Joan of Arc, along with biographical information and facts about the political and social forces that led to her being burned at the stake as a witch.
   ISBN 1-56006-466-8
   1. Joan, of Arc, Saint, 1412–1431—Juvenile literature. 2. Joan, of Arc, Saint, 1412–1431—Trials, litigation, etc.— Juvenile literature. 3. Hundred Years' War, 1339–1453— Juvenile literature. 4. Christian women saints—France— Biography—Juvenile literature. 5. France—History— Charles VII, 1422–1451—Juvenile literature. [1. Joan, of Arc, Saint, 1412–1431. 2. Joan, of Arc, Saint, 1412–1431—Trials, litigation, etc. 3. Saints. 4. Women–Biography. 5. France— History—Charles VII, 1422–1451.]
   I. Title. II. Series.
DC103.5.N37   1998
944'.026—DC21   97-9871
                                                                              CIP
                                                                               AC

Copyright © 1998 by Lucent Books, Inc.
P.O. Box 289011
San Diego, CA 92198-9011
Printed in the U.S.A.

Table of Contents

Foreword   4

Introduction
God's Grace or the Devil's Mischief?   7

Chapter 1
Joan the Maiden   11

Chapter 2
Joan the Warrior   27

Chapter 3
Joan the Prisoner   42

Chapter 4
Joan the Defiant   57

Chapter 5
Joan the Condemned   71

Epilogue
Joan the Martyr   83

Timeline   88
For Further Reading   89
Works Consulted   91
Index   93
Picture Credits   96
About the Author   96

Foreword

"The law is not an end in and of itself, nor does it provide ends. It is preeminently a means to serve what we think is right."

William J. Brennan Jr.

THE CONCEPT OF JUSTICE AND THE RULE OF LAW are hallmarks of Western civilization, manifested perhaps most visibly in widely famous and dramatic court trials. These trials include such important and memorable personages as the ancient Greek philosopher Socrates, who was accused and convicted of corrupting the minds of his society's youth in 399 B.C.; the French maiden and military leader Joan of Arc, accused and convicted of heresy against the church in 1431; to former football star O.J. Simpson, acquitted of double murder in 1995. These and other well-known and controversial trials constitute the most public, and therefore most familiar, demonstrations of a Western legal tradition that dates back through the ages. Although no one is certain when the first law code appeared or when the first formal court trials were held, Babylonian ruler Hammurabi introduced the first known law code in about 1760 B.C. It remains unclear how this code was administered, and no records of specific trials have survived. What is clear, however, is that humans have always sought to govern behavior and define actions in terms of law.

Almost all societies have made laws and prosecuted people for going against those laws, but the question of which behaviors to sanction and which to censure has always been controversial and remains in flux. Some, such as Roman orator and legislator Cicero, argue that laws are simply applications of universal standards. Cicero believed that humanity would agree on what constituted illegal behavior and that human laws were a mere extension of natural laws. "True law is right reason in agreement with nature," he wrote,

4

world-wide in scope, unchanging, everlasting. . . . We may not oppose or alter that law, we cannot abolish it, we cannot be freed from its obligations by any legislature. . . . This [natural] law does not differ for Rome and for Athens, for the present and for the future. . . . It is and will be valid for all nations and all times.

Cicero's rather optimistic view has been contradicted throughout history, however. For every law made to preserve harmony and set universal standards of behavior, another has been born of fear, prejudice, greed, desire for power, and a host of other motives. History is replete with individuals defying and fighting to change such laws—and even to topple governments that dictate such laws. Abolitionists fought against slavery, civil rights leaders fought for equal rights, millions throughout the world have fought for independence—these constitute a minimum of reasons for which people have sought to overturn laws that they believed to be wrong or unjust. In opposition to Cicero, then, many others, such as eighteenth-century English poet and philosopher William Godwin, believe humans must be constantly vigilant against bad laws. As Godwin said in 1793:

Laws we sometimes call the wisdom of our ancestors. But this is a strange imposition. It was as frequently the dictate of their passion, of timidity, jealousy, a monopolizing spirit, and a lust of power that knew no bounds. Are we not obliged perpetually to renew and remodel this misnamed wisdom of our ancestors? To correct it by a detection of their ignorance, and a censure of their intolerance?

Lucent Books' *Famous Trials* series showcases trials that exemplify both society's praiseworthy condemnation of universally unacceptable behavior, and its misguided persecution of individuals based on fear and ignorance, as well as trials that leave open the question of whether justice has been done. Each volume begins by setting the scene and providing a historical context to show how society's mores influence the trial process and the verdict. Each book goes on to present a detailed and lively account of the trial, including liberal use of primary source material such as direct testimony, lawyers' summations, and contemporary and modern commentary. In addition, sidebars throughout the text create a broader context by presenting illuminating details about important points of law, information on key personalities, and important distinctions related to civil, federal, and criminal procedures. Thus, all of the primary and secondary source material included in both the text and the sidebars demonstrates to readers the sources and methods historians use to derive information and conclusions about such events.

Lastly, each *Famous Trials* volume includes one or more of the following comprehensive tools that motivate readers to pursue further reading and research. A timeline allows readers to see the scope of the trial at a glance, annotated bibliographies provide both sources for further research and a thorough list of works consulted, a glossary helps students with unfamiliar words and concepts, and a comprehensive index permits quick scanning of the book as a whole.

The insight of Oliver Wendell Holmes Jr., distinguished Supreme Court justice, exemplifies the theme of the *Famous Trials* series. Taken from *The Common Law*, published in 1881, Holmes remarked: "The life of the law has not been logic, it has been experience." That "experience" consists mainly in how laws are applied in society and challenged in the courts, a process resulting in differing outcomes from one generation to the next. Thus, the *Famous Trials* series encourages readers to examine trials within a broader historical and social context.

Introduction

God's Grace or the Devil's Mischief?

I N THE MORNING OF SATURDAY, February 24, 1431, the great stone fortress known as Bouvreuil castle—in the northern French town of Rouen on the Seine River—was alive with activity. More than the usual number of servants, cooks, and stable boys hurried to and fro and, as part of a tightened security policy, the castle's regular garrison of soldiers had been increased. Like their comrades in the surrounding countryside, these troops were mainly English, for at this moment in the long conflict between England and France that would later be called the Hundred Years' War, northern France was occupied and controlled by the English.

As had happened the two preceding days and would happen again day after day for some time to come, the guards watched an impressive assembly of well-known high church officials file across the fortress's drawbridge, through its large open courtyard, and into its imposing main hall. Most of these clerics were Burgundians, Frenchmen allied with the English against the rightful French king, Charles VII. From the main hall, the churchmen entered a small, candle-lit chamber and took their places at an array of tables and chairs that had been set up for an ecclesiastical, or church-administered, trial. More than forty in number, these so-called "assessors" had the task of observing the proceedings and offering comments and advice to the judge.

7

It was in the tower rising in the foreground of this artist's restoration of Rouen's famous fifteenth-century castle that Joan's captors threatened her with torture if she refused to admit her guilt.

That judge, Pierre Cauchon, bishop of Beauvais, a stern-looking man in his early sixties, was already in the room, conversing quietly with the official court notaries, or scribes.

Once everyone was seated, Cauchon signaled an attendant at the door and the chamber fell silent, gripped by an atmosphere of tense anticipation. A few seconds later, a detachment of guards led in the accused, a nineteen-year-old French maiden wearing men's clothing, who took a seat facing the judge and assessors. It was immediately plain to all that the largely hostile host of older males that surrounded her did not intimidate her but, rather, that her demeanor was fearless, her expression proud and defiant. Her name was Jeanne d'Arc, whom most people at the time referred to as "the Maid," or as La Pucelle, "the Virgin." Posterity would call her Joan of Arc.

Six years before, Joan claimed, she had begun to hear voices that identified themselves as the long-dead Christian saints Michael, Margaret, and Catherine. Supposedly, these saints had convinced the young girl that she must go to the aid of Charles VII and help him drive the English out of France. Early in 1429, after persuading Charles and his advisers to give her the chance, Joan had led the French forces to victory at Orléans and Patay and soon afterward had triumphantly escorted Charles into Reims, which had long been in English hands. In the battles and sieges that had followed, the Maid had continued to rally the French liberation forces and to frustrate the English and their Burgundian allies. In May 1430, however, the Burgundians had captured Joan and after imprisoning her for several months, had finally turned her over to the English.

The English believed that Joan was a witch who had defeated them by summoning up supernatural forces. English leaders wanted the Church to pronounce her a heretic, or nonbeliever, so that they could publicly burn her, which, they hoped, would both demoralize the French armies and discredit Charles VII. Cauchon, who openly supported the English-Burgundian cause and who hated Joan for having recently driven him and his sympathizers out of Reims, had been chosen to conduct the trial; and he had made it his objective to find her guilty and condemn her, no matter what evidence might be presented.

With this objective in mind, on this Saturday morning Cauchon and one of his chief interrogators, Jean Beaupère, decided to question Joan about her voices. Their aim was to show that these voices she claimed to hear had been sent by the Devil to do evil mischief, and not by God to do good, as she so steadfastly maintained. "This voice which you say appears to you," asked Beaupère, "is it an angel or does it come directly from God?"

"This voice comes from God," Joan insisted, "and I think I shall not tell you fully what I know [about the voices]. I have a greater fear of being at fault by saying something which displeases these voices than I have of not answering you." This was only one of many instances in which the Maid surprised her accusers with her presence of mind and eloquence and frustrated them by cleverly evading their attempts to make her incriminate herself.

But a few minutes later Beaupère set a trap he was sure this uneducated and inexperienced young girl could not escape. "Are you in God's grace?" he queried. It was clear to everyone

*In this modern painting by artist Frederick Rae, Joan stands before her
accusers while court scribes (behind the table) record the proceedings.*

present that if she answered yes, she would be guilty of the sin
of pride and of presuming to speak for God; if, on the other
hand, she answered no, it would be an admission that God had
rejected her, that she was a sinner and perhaps even a nonbeliever. Hearing this seemingly unanswerable question, Cauchon
must have felt confident that the girl would stumble, prove her
guilt, and bring the trial to a speedy conclusion.

But any confidence Cauchon and the others may have felt
was soon swept away. With a simple but exceedingly clever
answer, Joan managed neatly to avoid Beaupère's trap, to draw
an astonished gasp from those gathered, and to put her accusers
on notice that the process of condemning her, if successful,
would be a long and difficult one.

Chapter 1

Joan the Maiden

BEFORE THE BIRTH OF JOAN OF ARC—whose turbulent life and tragic but heroic death would one day inspire and galvanize the forces of French nationalism—France was a divided, war-torn land. The so-called Hundred Years' War, which was in reality closer to a century and a half in duration, had begun with intermittent skirmishes between France and England in the 1290s. More serious and destructive warfare erupted a generation later. In 1328 England's king Edward III laid claim to the French throne on the basis of his mother's relationship as sister to the French king Charles IV, and in the following decade tensions between the two countries rapidly mounted.

The war finally exploded with full force in 1339, as Edward launched an invasion of France through Flanders (a medieval principality encompassing sections of what are now France, Belgium, and the Netherlands), with which he had allied himself; and, thereafter, succeeding monarchs on both sides continued to dispute and challenge one another. The most intense and destructive phases of the on-again, off-again conflict were those from 1340 to 1360, 1369 to 1389, and 1415 to 1435. Despite periodic victories by each of the opposing forces, the struggle dragged on and on, partly because the actual military clashes were largely sporadic and small-scale. This made it difficult for one side to score a massive, strategic knockout blow. Medieval scholar Frances Gies explains:

> The Hundred Years' War was characteristically medieval in its military aspect, dominated by sieges and raids.

11

Pitched battles were extreme rarities; in the thousand
years of the Middle Ages scarcely a dozen battles of memorable importance are recorded. When they occurred,
however, battles were typically bloody and tactically decisive, with the defeated army more or less wiped out.
Crécy, the first large battle of the Hundred Years' War, in
1346, was marked by the striking success of English
archers on foot, armed with powerful longbows, against
French mounted knights. In the second, Poitiers, in 1356,
the French tried to correct their tactics by dismounting to
attack, with equally disastrous results. Yet despite the
slaughter of numbers of French knights and lords, the two
battles had only limited strategic effect.

The castle of Broc looms in the distance in this depiction of the Battle of Crécy,
in which the English longbowmen won the day.

TRIUMPH OF THE LONGBOWS AT CRÉCY

The first major battle of the Hundred Years' War, at Crécy in 1346, was also the first known military engagement in which a new weapon, the English longbow, proved superior to traditional medieval configurations of mounted knights and crossbowmen. This vivid account of the battle is from fourteenth-century French historian Jean Froissart's *Chronicles* (as translated by John Bourchier in *The Chronicles of Froissart*).

The Englishmen, who were in three battles [regiments] lying on the ground to rest them, as soon as they saw the Frenchmen approach, they rose upon their feet . . . and arranged their battles. The first was the prince's [Edward the Black Prince's] battle. . . . The earl of Northampton and the earl of Arundel with the second battle were on the wing in good order, ready to comfort [aid] the prince's battle, if need were [while the third regiment, commanded by the king, Edward III, remained in reserve]. The lords and knights of France came not to engagement together in good order, for some came before and some came after, in such evil order that one of them did trouble [get in the way of] another. . . . When the Genoese [archers from the Italian kingdom of Genoa who fought as mercenaries for the French] were assembled together and began to approach [the English lines] they uttered a great cry to abash [startle and frighten] the Englishmen, but these stood still and stirred not for all that. Then the Genoese a second time made a fell cry and stept forward a little, but the Englishmen removed [retreated] not one foot. . . . Then they [the Genoese] shot fiercely with their crossbows. Then the English archers stepped forth one pace and let fly their arrows so wholly and so thick that it seemed [like] snow. When the Genoese felt the arrows piercing through their heads, arms and breasts, many of them cast down their crossbows. . . . When the French king saw them fly away he said, "Slay these rascals, for they shall . . . trouble us without reason.". . . Ever still the Englishmen shot where they saw the thickest press [of enemy soldiers]. The sharp arrows ran into the men-at-arms and into their horses, and many fell, horses and men . . . and when they were down they could not rise again. . . . And also among the Englishmen there were certain rascals that went afoot with great knives, and they went in among the [fallen French] men-at-arms and slew . . . many as they lay on the ground, both earls, barons, knights and squires.

Indeed, the entire twenty years constituting the first phase of the war did little more than confirm England's possession of Calais, on the English Channel in northern France, and a strip of southwestern France. A truce concluded in 1360 provided only a brief respite and the fighting resumed in 1369.

Relations between the warring parties took on a new dimension in the early 1400s. France's king Charles VI suffered from a severe mental illness that produced episodes of memory loss and violent behavior; and his unstable and weak rule allowed the kingdom to split into two opposing factions—known as the Burgundians and Armagnacs—each of which claimed the right to run the country in the king's name. Open civil war broke out in 1411 as John the Fearless, leader of the Burgundians, seized control of Paris and the national government.

A Simple, Good, and Pious Young Girl

It was into this troubled, war-ravaged France that Joan of Arc was born in 1412, barely a year after the commencement of civil strife. "In my town they called me Jeannette," she recalled later at her trial. In her own words, she described her upbringing:

> I was born in the town of Domrémy [on the Meuse River in northeastern France] which makes one with [the town of] Greux. It is in the place of Greux that the principal church is. My father was called Jacques d'Arc and my mother Isabelle. [I was baptized] in the church of Domrémy. . . . It was from my mother that I learnt Pater Noster [the Lord's Prayer], Ave Maria [Hail Mary], and Credo [the Apostles' Creed]. Nobody taught me my belief if not my mother. . . . [As a child, I learned] to sew linen cloths and to spin; for spinning and sewing let me alone [to compete] against any woman in Rouen. . . . When I was in my father's house, I busied myself with the housework.

Later recollections by some of those who knew Joan in Domrémy provide more details of her family life, daily activities, and character. For example, Jean Moreau, who had a farm in Greux, remembered that the d'Arcs were "good Catholics" and hard workers, as well as decent, sociable neighbors whom he enjoyed conversing with from time to time. Joan, he recalled, was extremely "well and properly brought up" and conducted herself so well that all of the residents of her village were very fond of her. "Jeannette," testified Moreau, was of seemly converse [could express herself well] so far as a girl of her condition [background] can be, for her parents were not very rich. And in her youth and until the time when she left her father's house, she went to the fields to plow and sometimes guarded the animals in the fields, and did women's work, spinning and the rest. Jeannette would go often and of her own will to the church . . . of Notre Dame de Bermont near to the town of Domrémy, when her parents thought that she was plowing or working elsewhere in the fields.

Simonin Musnier, one of Joan's childhood playmates, also remembered her fondly. As an adult, Musnier recalled that he had lived next door to the d'Arcs and knew Joan to be a simple, good, and pious young girl who gave whatever she could to those poorer than she and often cared for sick neighbors. "I myself was sick," said Musnier, "and Joan came to comfort me." Another childhood friend, Hauviette de Syonne, added the following:

Joan worked just like other young girls. She did the household chores, she spun, and sometimes—I have seen her—she watched her father's flocks. . . . I have been with Joan . . . who was my friend, and other girls and boys to the Fairies' Tree [around which, according to local legends, fairies used to dance] on Fountains Sunday [the fourth Sunday in Lent]. We used to eat there and dance and play.

Many of Joan's other friends and acquaintances offered similar testimony that as a young girl she was warmhearted, devout, hardworking, intelligent, and resourceful.

The English-Burgundian Alliance

That Joan's first few years were relatively peaceful and happy was due largely to the fact that the fighting and pillaging associated with the French civil war had not yet penetrated into the region in which she lived. But as she grew older, a series of political and military events caused the war to broaden in scope,

FONDLY REMEMBERING JOAN

In 1455, at the age of eighty, Beatrice d'Estelin, one of Joan's godmothers, gave the following fond remembrances (quoted from *The Retrial of Joan of Arc*) about Joan's childhood.

Joan was well and properly instructed in the Catholic faith like other girls of her age. And from her childhood and her adolescence up to her leaving her father's house she was brought up to good habits. She was chaste and well-mannered, and frequent and pious in her attendance at church and the holy shrines. And after the village of Domrémy was burnt [by the Burgundians in June 1428] Joan always went on saints' days to hear the Mass in the village of Greux; she confessed gladly on the proper days, and especially on the most holy feast day of Easter, or the Resurrection of Our Lord Jesus Christ. In my opinion there was not a better girl in the two villages. She applied herself to all the different jobs in her father's house, and sometimes she spun flax or wool, or went to the plow, or to the harvest fields, when it was time, and sometimes when it was her father's turn, she watched the village beasts or herds.

Young Joan tends sheep in the fields outside her native village of Domrémy.

bringing it ever closer to her home. Of these events, the first of major importance and impact involved France's longtime foe. Because of a truce concluded in 1389, England had not attacked France for some time; but English leaders had been keeping a keen eye on the escalating conflict between the Burgundians and Armagnacs. In 1415 England's king Henry V decided the time was right to take advantage of the political and civil chaos sweeping through France and he launched an invasion. After he landed his army at the mouth of the Seine River in August of that year, a large number of Burgundian and Armagnac lords and knights, for the moment putting the safety of the kingdom above their own differences, formed an uneasy alliance and marched north to halt his advance. In October the two armies clashed at Agincourt, south of Calais. According to historian Winston Churchill's account:

> The French, whose numbers have been estimated at about twenty thousand, were drawn up in three lines of battle, of which a proportion remained mounted. With justifiable confidence they awaited the attack of less than a third of their number, who, far from home and many marches from the sea, must win or die. . . . The [English] archers were disposed in six wedge-shaped formations, each supported by a body of men-at-arms. . . . The whole English army, even the King himself, dismounted and sent their horses to the rear; and shortly after eleven o'clock on St. Crispin's Day, October 25, he gave the order [to advance]. . . . The archers kissed the soil in reconciliation to God . . . and advanced to within three hundred yards of the heavy [French] masses in their front. They planted their stakes and loosed their arrows. . . . Under the arrow storm, [the French mounted knights] in their turn moved forward down the slope. . . . Still at thirty [rows] deep they felt sure of breaking the [English] line. But once again [as at Crécy and Poitiers] the long-bow destroyed all before it. [French] horse[men] and foot [soldiers] alike went down; a long heap of armored dead and wounded lay upon the ground, over which the reinforcements struggled bravely, but in vain. In this grand moment the archers slung their bows [aside], and, sword in hand, fell upon the reeling squadrons and disordered masses [of French troops].

In the two to three hours the battle lasted, more than ten thousand French died, while the English lost perhaps less than a tenth that number. This sweeping victory gave the English a

A *modern depiction of England's King Henry V fighting in the Battle of Agincourt, in which his forces won a decisive victory.*

strong foothold in northern France, a base from which to launch raids at will into French-held territory. In effect, the larger Hundred Years' War had resumed and in the process absorbed the smaller French civil conflict.

Soon Henry further solidified his position by making a secret pact with John the Fearless, who now recognized Henry and his descendants as legitimate heirs to the French throne. In the years that followed, this formidable English-Burgundian alliance appeared to spell doom for the nationalist Armagnac cause. Believing he had no other choice, in 1420 the weak, insane, and aging Charles VI agreed to the Treaty of Troyes, which named Henry as ruler over the "dual monarchy" of England and France. To seal the union of the two states, Henry married Charles's daughter Catherine.

But to the surprise of many, the alliance and treaty failed to extinguish the French nationalist cause. Partly to eliminate a possible claimant to the French throne, the Troyes agreement disinherited Charles VII, then in his teens, who bore the title of dauphin, meaning the French king's eldest son. The younger Charles had earlier fled to Bourges in central France, and there he now began

A *portrait of King Henry V dressed in formal court attire.*

to draw the support of many embittered Armagnacs, who refused to knuckle under to the English and Burgundians. After establishing a rival French court, Charles resumed the fighting, which now took the form of a war of liberation (or from his enemy's point of view, the putting down of a rebellion).

Two years later, in 1422, both Charles VI and Henry V died (Henry's death at age thirty-five, caused by dysentery, being quite unexpected), but the conflict raged on. As in earlier stages of the Hundred Years' War, the fighting largely consisted of small-scale raids and counterraids in which towns, villages, and farms were pillaged and burned. An English soldier of the time, one Captain John Fastolf, summed up and advocated the standard tactics, saying that his comrades should march through enemy territory,

> burning and destroying all the lands as they pass, both house, grain, vine, and all trees that bear fruit for man's sustenance, and all cattle that may not be driven, to be destroyed. . . . And it seems verily that by these ways and governance, the king shall conquer his realm of France, and harm and destroy his enemies and save his people and his soldiers.

The Voices and the Mission

Eventually some of the fighting reached the vicinity of Domrémy. In 1423 the husband of one of Joan's cousins was killed by a stone cannonball during the Burgundian siege of a nearby town. In that same year, Robert de Saarbruck, an unscrupulous local nobleman-turned-brigand, who frequently switched his allegiance from one warring faction to the other, demanded that the villagers of Domrémy pay him a hefty annual fee. In return, he promised to protect the village from roving raiders and to keep it immune from the war's effects. Out of fear for their lives and property, the villagers at first complied and paid de Saarbruck. But his so-called protection was nearly worthless, for in 1424 bands of soldier-brigands freely roamed the area; and in 1425 raiders carried away most of Domrémy's cattle, furniture, and other valuable assets. Luckily for the d'Arcs and their neighbors, a sympathetic local lord led his troops against these raiders and recovered the stolen goods.

At the time of the cattle raid—a clear signal to Domrémy's residents that the war had reached their doorstep—Joan was thirteen years old. It was during this crisis that she claimed she first began hearing voices, which identified themselves as those of angels and also the Christian saints Michael, Margaret, and Catherine. Whether these voices constituted actual miraculous visitations, or were instead delusions caused by extreme anxiety or some form of mental illness, will never be known. What is important and seems almost certain is that Joan sincerely believed that her voices came from God and that she had been given a divine mission to fulfill. About the nature of the voices and the mission, she later testified:

> When I was thirteen years old I had a voice from God to help me govern my conduct. And the first time I was very fearful. And came this voice, about the hour of noon, in the summertime, in my father's garden. . . . Rarely do I hear it without a brightness. . . . It is usually a great light. . . . The voice was sent to me by God and, after I had thrice [three times] heard this voice, I knew that it was the voice of an angel. . . . This voice told me, twice or thrice a week, that I, Joan, must go away and that I must come to France and that my father must know nothing of my leaving. . . . The voice told me that I should raise the siege laid to the city of Orléans [about seventy miles southwest of Paris]. The voice told me also that I should make my way to Robert de Baudricourt in the fortress of Vaucouleurs [north of Domrémy], the Captain of that place, that he would give me people to go with me. . . . [Saint Michael] told me to be a good child and that God would help me. And, among other things he told me to come to the help of the King of France [Charles VII, the dauphin].

Following the urgings of her voices, in May 1428 Joan, now sixteen, began the first leg of her preordained journey, the trek

In this modern painting, Joan listens intently to the voices she later claimed urged her to offer her services to Charles VII and to lift the siege of Orléans.

to the fortress of Vaucouleurs. In order to keep her parents from learning her destination, as the angel had commanded, she first obtained her father's permission to stay a few days at her cousin's home in a village near Vaucouleurs. During this visit, she convinced her cousin's husband, Durand Laxart, to take her to the fortress. "When I came to this town of Vaucouleurs," Joan later recalled, "I recognized Robert de Baudricourt, whereas never before had I seen him . . . for the [angelic] voice told me it was him." At first, de Baudricourt, thinking Joan a brash young dreamer, rejected her plea for him to take her to see the dauphin Charles and the disappointed young woman went home.

The war then quickly escalated, both in the surrounding region and across France. Only a month after Joan's visit with de Baudricourt, the Burgundians launched an offensive aimed at capturing his fortress at Vaucouleurs; and on their way toward their objective, these troops burned Domrémy and Greux, forcing the villagers to flee southward. The attempt to take Vaucouleurs failed, and the d'Arcs and their neighbors returned to Domrémy and started rebuilding. But at that very moment other Burgundian offensives were in motion, the largest one aimed at striking southward into Bourges and destroying the dauphin's nationalist forces. As part of this southward thrust, in October 1428 the Burgundians laid siege to the strategic city of Orléans on the Loire River.

Joan Meets the Dauphin

Fearing that the dauphin's cause might be lost if she did not help him, Joan felt pressed to make another appeal to Robert de Baudricourt, and in January 1429 she returned to Vaucouleurs, again without informing her parents. This time, after some considerable impassioned persuasion, she managed to win over de Baudricourt. In February he assigned a group of six armed men to escort her as quickly and stealthily as possible across hostile enemy territory to the dauphin's enclave at Chinon, about seventy miles west of Bourges.

To the surprise of many, including her companions, Joan won over Charles more easily than she had de Baudricourt. According to an eyewitness, after the young woman arrived at Chinon, but before the dauphin had met her,

> it was the King's [dauphin's] will that she be first examined by clerks and churchmen, which was done. And at last . . . it was decided that the King would listen to her . . . and Joan was granted an audience. When the

This painting, completed in 1918, less than two years before the Catholic Church made Joan a saint, shows her making her case to Robert de Baudricourt.

King knew that she was coming, he withdrew apart from the others [his nobles and courtiers]. Joan, however, knew him at once and made him a reverence and spoke to him for some time. After having heard her, the King appeared radiant. Thereafter . . . he sent her to Poitiers that she be examined by the clerks of the University of Poitiers. When he knew that she had been examined and it was reported to him that they had found nothing but what was good in her, the King had armor made for her and entrusted her to his men of war, and she was given command in the matter of war.

An old woodcut shows Joan (depicted at left, much too old and too elegantly dressed) confronting Charles VII (seated on throne) at Chinon.

JOAN AT THE COURT IN CHINON

One of the eyewitnesses to Joan's appearance at the dauphin Charles's court at Chinon was Jean d'Aulon, a knight who was then acting as one of Charles's advisers. D'Aulon, who subsequently became one of Joan's close associates, later gave this recollection (quoted from *The Retrial of Joan of Arc*) of some of her experiences at the court.

After her presentation the Maid talked with our lord the King [Charles] in private, and told him certain secrets which I do not know; except that shortly afterward my lord sent for some members of his Council, among them myself. He told us that the Maid had said that she was sent from God to help him to recover his kingdom, which at the time was largely occupied by the English, his ancient enemies. After this . . . it was decided to interrogate the Maid, who was then about sixteen years old, or thereabouts, on certain points touching her faith. For this purpose the King sent for certain masters of theology, jurists, and other experts, who examined and interrogated her on these points well and diligently. I was present at the Council when these scholars made their report . . . and it was publicly stated by one of them that they had neither seen, learnt of, nor become acquainted with anything in the Maid that should not be present in a good Christian and a true Catholic, which they considered her to be; and it was their opinion that she was a very good person. When the King had received the scholars' report, this Maid was put into the care of the . . . mother of the Queen . . . and of certain ladies who were with her. These ladies saw and visited the Maid, and . . . examined the privy [private] parts of her body. But after they had seen and examined . . . [her] the Queen said and told the King that she and her ladies had found her beyond any doubt to be a true and intact virgin, with no signs of corruption or violation. I was present when the Queen made her report.

Charles's motivation for giving this young maiden, whom he had never met before, what amounted to an honorary generalship in his army is uncertain. Perhaps he was so devoutly religious and superstitious that he readily accepted her voices as miraculous and their advice as God's will; or maybe, considering the present perilous situation with the English and Burgundians threatening from nearly all sides, he figured he had nothing to lose. Perhaps by letting Joan act as a figurehead for his troops he

An engraving from the January 1845 edition of Arthur's Magazine *depicts Joan in her famous and characteristic military garb.*

would be providing them with a symbol of French family and purity to rally behind, a potent visual reminder of what they were fighting and dying for. Whatever the dauphin's reasoning, his placing of the Maid at the forefront of his forces was a bold gamble that would soon pay off beyond his wildest expectations. In April 1429, in what was surely one of history's most unusual sights, the seventeen-year-old girl, with an army at her back and banners blazing, rode northward toward besieged Orléans and a date with destiny.

Chapter 2

Joan the Warrior

As Joan of Domrémy led the dauphin's army toward the besieged city of Orléans in late April 1429, she no doubt thought long and hard about the lofty and formidable goals she had set for herself. First among these was to force the English and Burgundians to lift the siege of Orléans. Then, also in accordance with the will of her voices, she would help the Armagnac forces drive the enemy farther northward until the city of Reims had been liberated. Reims, located about 135 miles northeast of Paris, was France's traditional site of royal coronations. No matter how much Charles might protest that as Charles VI's eldest son he was the rightful king, most of the French would not accept the validity of that claim unless he, the dauphin, was crowned in the time-honored way at Reims. And at the moment that city lay in English-controlled territory, guarded by a Burgundian garrison of soldiers. Joan seemed confident that once Charles had been crowned, making his claim to the kingship official, a majority of the French would rise up and sweep the English out of France.

Joan must also have been aware that her own credibility would be a key factor in fulfilling these grandiose and optimistic goals. Political and military success would clearly require that the French—especially the army generals, but also the rank-and-file soldiers and general civilian populace—believe that her mission was really divinely inspired. And they would also need to accept the feasibility of a young girl with no military training leading an army to victory; since such a feat would be seen as a miracle, Joan's success depended in large degree on a wide-

27

spread belief in miracles. Luckily for her, she lived in an era when both religious faith and superstition were profoundly powerful forces in society. As scholar Régine Pernoud puts it, "We must enter into the general mentality of the period. Everybody at that time . . . believed in God, and in a God who was master of all eventualities and could, therefore, intervene at will to make the unexpected happen: in other words, everyone believed in miracles." Indeed, Joan's friend Jean d'Aulon remarked after her death, "All the Maid's exploits seemed to me rather divine and miraculous than otherwise. It would have been impossible for anyone as young as the Maid to perform such deeds except at the will and guidance of Our Lord." A corresponding and equally strong belief in the dark side of the divine, namely the Devil and witchcraft, would eventually be used against Joan in her trial; but for the moment, as she marched toward Orléans, many French saw her as God's champion.

Entry into Orléans

In fact, the rumor that God had sent a young maiden to liberate France rapidly spread northward ahead of the army. Many villagers congregated on the roadsides to see the troops pass by and hopefully catch a glimpse of the Maid, who must have presented a highly uncommon, yet splendid and impressive sight in her full battle array. According to d'Aulon, whom Charles had appointed as her guard and escort, "To protect her body, my lord the King had armor made exactly to fit her, and when that was done he picked out a certain number of soldiers to lead and escort her carefully." Among these escorts, in addition to d'Aulon, were Joan's brothers, Jean and Pierre, also decked out in armor, and a squire and two pages. Completing the colorful and heroic image projected by Joan and her entourage, above them floated a large banner that she had ordered made to her exact specifications; on its white background a gold fleur-de-lys, the symbol of lily flowers associated with the French crown, was emblazoned, along with images of Jesus and the archangels Michael and Gabriel.

As Joan and her followers approached Orléans on April 29, 1429, the city's predicament became apparent. It was situated on

NEARLY IMPREGNABLE TOWN DEFENSES

In this excerpt from their book *Daily Life in the Middle Ages*, scholars Clara and Richard Winston describe the formidable fortifications that protected large medieval towns like Orléans, making besieging them a bloody and sometimes protracted business.

The new walls built around French towns were well-nigh impregnable. They were very thick, with an inside and outside course of stone and rubble between. Topping the walls were battlements—tall stone curbs behind which bowmen could crouch to shoot their arrows through narrow apertures [openings]. At intervals the walls were supplemented by towers. Bounding up the staircases inside these towers, the defenders could quickly and safely reach the top of the walls and be ready to grapple with an attacking party. Stones were hurled and boiling water poured down as the attackers struggled up their ladders. The entrances into the towns were shielded by gates and heavy metal grills called portcullises. There was also a drawbridge raised and lowered by pulleys. Walls were further protected by a wide, deep moat. This could be filled with water brought from a nearby stream via canal or be left dry and allowed to grow up to rough briers. Perpetual watch was kept from the high towers flanking the principal gate, and the town was locked up every night even in peaceful times.

This drawing of the siege of Orléans shows the city's defensive battlements and towers, which long held back the attacking English forces.

the northern bank of the Loire and its main bridge was blocked by English forces holding a nearby fortress called the Tourelles. All of the other bridges in the area were also in English hands, as was the church of St. Loup, on the northeastern approach to the city. Luckily for the locals, the church lay over a mile from the city walls and the besiegers could not constantly police all of the open land between; hence, messengers and small groups of people were often able to make it in and out of Orléans through this no-man's-land. However, the only practical approach for large-scale relief was along the river, on which barges of supplies could be floated downstream to the city's docks. Therefore, the first order of business for Joan's army when it reached the Loire was to float boats loaded with provisions down to the beleaguered town.

But at that moment Orléans's French commander, Jean Dunois, wanted more than supplies. After rowing upstream to meet Joan, Dunois was duly impressed with her and felt it paramount that she enter the city immediately to raise the people's spirits. That night, at about eight o'clock, he, Joan, and a number of lords, captains, and soldiers brazenly rode along the city's northeastern approach and made a triumphant entrance, while the English garrison in the church at St. Loup, for whatever reason, made no attempt to stop them. According to the anonymous chronicle known as the *Journal of the Siege of Orléans*, Joan

> entered [the city] armed at all points, riding upon a white horse; and she caused her standard to be borne before her. . . . She entered thus into Orléans, having on her left hand [Dunois] very richly armed and mounted, and after came many other noble and valiant lords, esquires, captains, and men of war . . . and likewise some burgesses [leading citizens] of Orléans who had gone out to meet her. On the other hand came to receive her the other men of war, burgesses and matrons of Orléans, bearing great plenty of torches and making such rejoicing as if they had seen God descend in their midst; and not without cause, for they had many cares . . . and great fear lest they . . . lose all, body and goods [to the English]. But they felt themselves

already comforted and as if no longer besieged, by the divine virtue which they were told was in this simple maid, who looked upon them all right affectionately. . . . And there was a marvelous crowd and press to touch her or the horse upon which she was. So much so that one of those bearing a torch drew so near to her standard that the pennon took fire. Wherefore she struck spurs to her horse and turned him right gently towards the pennon and extinguished the fire . . . as if she had long served in the wars; which thing the men-at-arms held a great marvel.

Joan, holding her famous banner, is received by enthusiastic crowds during her triumphant entry into besieged Orléans.

Indeed God's Messenger

During the next few days, Joan and the other French commanders prepared a military strategy that they hoped would break
the English siege. Joan apparently thought it was worth the
attempt first to threaten the enemy into leaving, and she com-
posed and sent letters stating her demands to the English commanders. The third and last of these dispatches, which has
survived, reads in part:

> You, Englishmen, who have no right in this Kingdom of
> France, the King of Heaven orders and commands you
> through me, Joan the Maid, that you quit your fortresses
> and return into your own country, or if not I shall make
> you . . . [so much trouble] that the memory of it will be
> perpetual. That is what I write to you for the third and
> last time, and shall write no more.

Joan attached the letter to an arrow and had an archer fire it into
the English compound at Tourelles, all the while screaming
loudly to them, "Here's news for you! Read it!" As in the case of
her prior letters, the English response consisted of rude remarks
and taunts, some calling Joan the "Armagnacs' whore," and others saying she should go back to tending her cows. From the
English point of view, their siege was well mounted and bound
to succeed and the Maid was nothing more than an impudent
upstart who was in no position to issue them demands.

However, succeeding events soon took the English by surprise and quickly deflated their swagger and overconfidence. On
May 4 Dunois led a force out of the city and attacked the church
at St. Loup; and later in the day Joan charged a troop of reinforcements into the fray. On seeing the young girl fearlessly
throw herself into the midst of the fighting in what they knew
was her first battle, the soldiers in Dunois's regiment sent up a
rousing cheer and renewed the assault with ferocious vigor. The
attack was so overwhelming that the English garrison soon surrendered, suffering 114 killed and 40 captured.

Emboldened by this victory, which shocked and embarrassed
the English, in the days that followed the French forces launched

one devastating sortie after another. On May 6 Joan led four thousand men against the Tourelles fortress; and on this occasion, according to one fifteenth-century chronicle, she was wounded in the foot by a spiked metal ball. When this large French force failed to break through the massive enemy defenses, it attacked again the next day. This time the assault was even more furious and bloody, with the French employing scaling ladders and every weapon at their disposal. Joan was wounded again, this time by an

This well-known painting by nineteenth-century French artist Jules Eugène Lenepveu captures a dramatic moment from the siege of Orléans.

Wounded in the shoulder by an English arrow during furious fighting outside Orléans's walls, Joan steadfastly refused to retire from the battle.

arrow in the shoulder, but remained on the field, shouting orders and encouragements to her men, who were now thoroughly convinced that she must indeed be God's messenger. At the end of the day, after large numbers of English had died (over four hundred drowning in the river when a drawbridge collapsed), the fortress surrendered.

That night, Dunois later recalled, "I came in again, as also the Maid, with the other French, into the city of Orléans, in which we were received with great transports of joy and piety. And Joan was taken to her lodgings that her wound might be dressed." The army physicians no doubt did everything they could to keep her on her feet, for the troops now saw her as an indispensable morale booster who, at all costs, must be present on the field the next day.

And sure enough, to everyone's relief, on May 8 she appeared at the head of the army, riding her trademark white stallion and carrying her striking banner, flanked by Dunois and the other commanders. This time, however, no battle ensued. Instead, the overjoyed French watched as the English abandoned their remaining forts. Jean d'Aulon later recalled that the enemy "raised the siege and departed, discomfited [frustrated] and in confusion. And so, thanks to the help of Our Lord and the Maid, the city was delivered from the hands of the enemy."

The Road to Reims

The news of Orléans's delivery from the English siege rapidly spread across France. Most astonishing to all, especially the English leaders, was that the daring exploits of a "mere maid" had proved the deciding factor in the French victory. The English and Burgundians were now convinced more than ever that Joan must be some kind of sorceress, while French nationalists and their sympathizers took great heart and looked forward to the Armagnac army going on the offensive and marching northward to liberate enemy-held cities.

The nationalists were not disappointed in this respect. Joan and the army commanders left Orléans on May 9 and were soon joined by one of the dauphin Charles's relatives—twenty-five-year-old Jean, duke of Alençon, whom Charles had just commissioned as a "lieutenant general." Alençon had earlier met and become enraptured by Joan at Chinon and was delighted at the chance to serve with her. He must have been exceedingly grateful as well when, during their first battle together, she saved his life. The first phase of the new French offensive was the so-called Loire campaign, the objective of which was to liberate some of

Orléans's sister towns along that river. In the opening salvo, the Armagnacs stormed Jargeau, southeast of Orléans, on June 12, 1429, and during the intense fighting, as Alençon later recollected,

> Joan told me at one moment to retire from the place where I was standing, for if I did not "that engine"—and she pointed to a piece of artillery in the town—"will kill you." I fell back, and a little later on that very spot where I had been standing someone by the name of my lord de Lude was killed.

Alençon recorded many other details of the lightning campaign. First, Jargeau fell in a single day to the French, who, leaving over eleven hundred dead Englishmen in their wake, immediately marched on and laid siege to Beaugency, located

At the Battle of Patay, fancifully pictured here, the English suffered a disastrous defeat, losing at least one-third of their forces.

southwest of Orléans. Unable or unwilling to withstand the assault, Beaugency's English garrison, which had earlier retreated into the town's central fortress, surrendered about June 16. Two days later, at Patay, northwest of Orléans, Joan's army clashed with a large English force that had been sent to destroy it, or at least to prevent it from moving any farther northward. When the French took the enemy by surprise, the English commander, Sir John Fastolf, fled the field, abandoning his men, who then fell into confusion and suffered a horrendous defeat. At least a third of the English army of about six thousand was wiped out, while the French lost a mere three soldiers!

The costly and embarrassing losses in the Loire valley, especially at Patay, left the English and Burgundians with insufficient military manpower to defend and hold all of northern France, so the French encountered little opposition as they marched northeastward. Joan's army took the town of Troyes, on the Seine River over a hundred miles northeast of Orléans, on July 10. Then these forces, by now brimming with vigor and confidence, swung due north toward their ultimate goal, the coronation city of Reims. There, hearing that the Maid and her troops were approaching, and realizing that the vast majority of the townspeople sympathized with the Armagnac cause, the soldiers of the Burgundian garrison prudently fled while they could.

On July 16 Joan and the dauphin Charles rode side by side in a triumphant entry into the city, which had gladly opened its gates to them. In addition to the overjoyed crowds of townspeople that swarmed about them, they were met by several local Burgundian lords, who thereby renounced their allegiance to the English and joined the nationalists. The next day, in fulfillment of Joan's promise to deliver the dauphin to Reims for coronation, she proudly knelt beside him as he was officially crowned Charles VII, the "Lord's anointed," the legitimate king of France.

The Maid's Last Campaign

No sooner had Joan completed this phase of her mission, than she embarked on another. While in Reims, she wrote to the powerful duke of Burgundy, urging him to consider a peace plan that

THE ENGLISH DISASTER AT PATAY

This is part of the fifteenth-century Burgundian chronicler Jean de Wavrin's account of the confusion among the English units in the woods near Patay that led to their disastrous rout at the hands of the French (quoted from the English translation in Pernoud's *Joan of Arc by Herself and Her Witnesses*).

The English lords sent riding certain of their men who at once returned and related that the French were coming swiftly after them, riding in great strength, and so they were seen coming a little time thereafter. It was ordered by our Captains that those of the van-guard [the foremost military units] . . . should go forward to take up a position all along by the woods which were near Patay. This thing was so done. . . . Tensely came the French after their enemy, whom they could not yet see nor knew the place where they were, when it happened that their skirmishers saw a stag come out of the woods, which . . . plunged into the midst of the English regiment whence [from which] arose a great cry, for they knew not that their enemy was so close to them. . . . When, then, the English saw the French draw so near, they hurried as much as they could in order to reach the woods before their coming, but they were able to accomplish only so much. . . . And then, [seeing] Sir John Fastolf [an English commander] riding towards the van-guard to join up with them, those of the van-guard thought that all was lost and that the men of the regiment were in flight. Hence, the captain of the van-guard . . . took flight and abandoned the woods. Hence, Sir John Fastolf, seeing the danger of this flight, knowing that all was going very badly, had the notion of saving himself. . . . And finally the English were there undone at small loss to the French.

would unite the long-embittered opposing French forces. Joan must have felt certain that in the face of total French solidarity, the English would surely withdraw altogether from France. The Maid's mood brightened considerably when Burgundy soon agreed to a fifteen-day truce, at the same time hinting that he might give up control of Paris; however, it quickly became evident that this was just a ruse designed to buy time for the arrival of English reinforcements.

Feeling used and betrayed, an angry Joan now advocated marching directly on Paris, and in anticipation of an attack, the Parisians fortified the city. The anticipated assault came on September 8,

1429, exactly four months after the lifting of the siege of Orléans, with Joan, Alençon, and the other French officers once more leading the way. Alençon's chronicler, Perceval de Cagny, later recorded:

> The attack was hard and long and it was a marvel to hear the noise and din of the cannon . . . which those within [the city] fired at those without, and all manner of missiles in such great abundance as to be innumerable. . . . The assault lasted from about the hour of noon, to about the hour of nightfall, and after sunset the Maid was struck by a cross-bow bolt in the thigh. And since being struck forced herself to cry louder than ever that every man should approach the walls and that the place would be taken.

But to Joan's great regret, the French failed to take Paris. The city's defenders, most of them staunch Burgundians, had managed to repel the first day's attack, in the process inflicting over a thousand Armagnac casualties. This convinced the king that it

This fanciful woodcut of Joan (far left) at the siege of Paris incorrectly depicts her wearing a dress instead of armor.

THE BENEFITS AND DRAWBACKS OF MEDIEVAL ARMOR

In this excerpt from his book *The Art of War in the Western World*, military historian Archer Jones discusses changes in the armored suits of medieval knights just prior to and during the era of the Hundred Years' War. His description of a knight's difficulty in remounting after being unhorsed calls to mind Joan's predicament at Compiègne after an enemy soldier had pulled her from her mount.

In the thirteenth century armored men began to use [metal] plates to strengthen their mail armor [made of flexible, overlapping metal scales] at particularly vulnerable points, such as the shin and knee. Gradually heavy cavalry added more and more plate . . . until a complete suit of plate armor, which protected the wearer from the shock of blows and deflected both hand weapons and crossbow bolts, became common. A helmet that completely covered the face had already been adopted. A suit of the new armor could weigh seventy pounds, and, together with its own armor, the horse had to carry over 100 pounds of metal alone. With a horse protected from lance wounds in the chest and the rider virtually proof against harm, the knight became far more formidable. However, this alteration both raised the cost of the mounted man and seriously reduced his mobility.

A full suit of armor from the fifteenth century, the period in which Joan fought the English. Such outfits protected the wearers well but were heavy and inflexible.

The heavier burdened horse found it harder to gallop and the rider had difficulty in executing any maneuver but the straight-ahead charge. Dismounted, the rider could walk only with difficulty and had trouble climbing onto his horse and rising if he fell.

would be unwise to make any more forays against such a large and well-fortified city, and he ordered his army to withdraw toward the Loire. He expressed the hope that Paris might be taken with less bloodshed at some future date.

Joan spent most of winter with Charles in the Loire region. During these months, probably in late December 1429, he repaid her loyalty and courage by ennobling her, her family, and their heirs, in effect making them all members of the French nobility. Thereafter, their honorary family name was "du Lys," after the fleur-de-lys on Joan's banner, and their coat of arms bore a sword supporting a crown, flanked by two golden fleurs-de-lys.

In the spring it became necessary for new French campaigns in the north. The duke of Burgundy moved on Compiègne, northeast of Paris, in March 1430, and Joan marshaled a force to oppose him, arriving at the embattled city on May 14. Here, her long string of courageous battlefield exploits finally ended. During a wild assault on an enemy force vastly superior in numbers, she was unhorsed, and, partly because of the weight and inflexibility of her armor, could not remount; as a result she was taken prisoner, along with Jean d'Aulon and her brothers Pierre and Jean. A Burgundian observer recorded:

> Fortune allowed that her glory at last come to an end and that she bear arms no longer; an archer, a rough man and a sour, full of spite because of a woman . . . [who had] overthrown so many valiant men, dragged her to one side by her . . . cloak and pulled her from her horse, throwing her flat on the ground; never could she find recourse . . . in her men, try though [they] might to remount her [on her horse].

Joan's captors handed her over to the Burgundian captain John of Luxembourg, who took her to his camp at Claroix, not far north of Compiègne; and there began the long and arduous ordeal of imprisonment that preceded her trial and martyrdom.

Chapter 3

Joan the Prisoner

AFTER SHE WAS CAPTURED by the Burgundians and taken into John of Luxembourg's custody, Joan became a highly coveted prize of war, especially to the English. John was not an English subject but an ally, and therefore he was not obliged to deliver his prisoner directly into English hands; rather, he had the right to exchange, ransom, or hold on to her at his pleasure. So English leaders negotiated an agreement whereby John would turn Joan over to them in exchange for a hefty ransom of ten thousand gold francs. It took several months to raise the money, and in the meantime Joan's captor shuffled her from one location to another. In December 1430, after the ransom was paid, English authorities finally took Joan into their custody and brought her to Rouen, the capital city of Normandy, which was at the time, both politically and culturally, the most English section of France.

The English clearly feared Joan, both as a supposed witch who could summon supernatural forces against them on the battlefield and as a symbol behind which the French nationalists might continue to rally; therefore, English leaders were eager to get rid of her. But because of her widespread notoriety, it was important that they first discredit her popular image as an instrument of God. By publicly proving that she was, instead, a witch and a heretic, they hoped to eliminate any chance that in death she might become a martyr to their enemies' cause.

To establish Joan's heresy, the English relied on the Church, in this case local Burgundian church officials with whom they were allied, and more specifically the Inquisition. This was a judicial wing of the Roman Catholic Church that had been created in the thirteenth century to help root out and prosecute heretics in Italy and France and that eventually spread to other parts of Europe. The Inquisition's courts were not allowed to pronounce the death penalty—punishments for people who admitted their guilt ranged from whippings and monetary fines to imprisonment; however, the Church's courts turned those who refused to repent over to the secular authorities, who almost always executed them, usually by burning them at the stake. The English hoped that Joan's case would follow this last scenario and that she would be burned to ashes and forgotten.

Like other trials conducted by the Inquisition, Joan's was very different from those that took place in secular courts. There were no lawyers or juries. The assessors, usually noted and learned churchmen, attended proceedings as advisers to the judge (or judges), and although they could ask the suspect questions, they had no authority to pass sentence. The role of chief judge belonged to the main Inquisitor, who was also the prosecutor charged with the task of questioning the suspect about his or her activities, beliefs, and even thoughts. And he was in addition a

An old woodcut shows a general session of the Inquisition court. Unlike modern secular trials, such proceedings featured no lawyers or juries.

kind of father confessor, for the Church considered it paramount to save the guilty person's soul. Unlike the rule in most modern law courts, the accused was not presumed innocent until proven guilty. Scholar W. S. Scott explains:

> The prisoner was not charged with an offense of which the promoter [prosecutor] had to find him guilty. On the contrary, no specific charges were brought against him in the beginning. He was merely questioned in the hope that he might admit some offense. On his replies the promoter formulated the charges in the form of Articles. These Articles were then put to the prisoner, and it was for him to refute them. He was in fact considered guilty unless he could prove himself innocent.

The first stage of Joan's trial, in which she was questioned repeatedly so that her judges could formulate the Articles against her, lasted over a month and produced a number of dramatic exchanges between the prisoner and her questioners.

A Lack of Objectivity and Fairness

The partisan, biased, and mean-spirited tone of this initial phase of the trial, like that of the later phases, was set by the chief Inquisitor, Pierre Cauchon, bishop of Beauvais. Cauchon, whose fruitful career had included work as a diplomat and as rector of the University of Paris in addition to his religious duties, was a staunch supporter of the English-Burgundian alliance and was, therefore, hostile toward Joan from the outset. Like most of his Burgundian and English friends and colleagues, he was already convinced before the trial began that she was a witch and a heretic, and he zealously set out to prove this publicly by whatever means were necessary.

Cauchon's lack of objectivity and fairness is illustrated in the way he conducted pretrial inquiries about Joan's life, a routine Inquisition procedure. Sending agents to Domrémy and other places she had frequented to gather information about her, he hoped to uncover all manner of suspicious and damning former acts and statements that could be used against her in the trial. Not surprisingly, when the agents returned with nothing incriminating, he was furious. A Rouen merchant named Jean Moreau testified later:

> I know that at the time when Joan was in Rouen and they were preparing a trial against her, someone important from the country [region] of Lorraine came to Rouen. As I was of the same country I made his acquaintance. He told me that he had come from Lorraine to Rouen because he had been especially commissioned to gather information in Joan's country of origin to learn what reputation she had there. Which he had done. And he had reported his information to the lord Bishop of Beauvais, thinking to have compensation for his work and his expenses; but the bishop told him he was a traitor and a bad man and that he had not done what he should have done and was ordered to do. This man complained of it to me for, from what he said, he could not get his salary paid him because his informations were not useful to the bishop. He added that in the course of collecting his informations he had found nothing concerning Joan which he would not have liked to find about his own sister, although he had been for information to five or six parishes near Domrémy and in that town itself.

Meanwhile, Joan—who languished in a prison cell in Rouen, constantly chained for fear she might escape or try to harm herself—was examined to find out if she was a virgin, as she staunchly claimed to be. Jean Fabri, one of the assessors at the trial, later recalled:

> I know well that once, when Joan was asked why she was called the Maid and whether she was one, she answered: "I can well say that I am so, and if you do not believe me have me examined by some women." And she declared herself ready to suffer this examination provided it be done by decent women, as is the custom.

It is important to understand that in Joan's day any unmarried woman who had engaged in sexual relations was looked upon as

JOAN IN CHAINS

In this excerpt from the testimony he gave many years after Joan's death (quoted from *The Retrial of Joan of Arc*), Jean Massieu, the usher at her original trial, describes the cruel treatment she endured in the months she was imprisoned in Rouen.

I know for certain that at night she lay chained by the legs with two pairs of irons, and tightly secured by another chain which passed through the legs of her bed, and was attached to a great block of wood five or six foot long, by means of a lock. In this way she was unable to stir from her place. . . . As for her prison, Joan was in a room in the center of Rouen castle, approached by eight stairs. . . . There were five English guards of the lowest sort, whom we should describe in French as common torturers, to watch her. And they were most eager for Joan's death, and often mocked her; and she reproached them for it. And I have heard from Étienne Castille, the blacksmith, that he made an iron cage for her, in which she was held in a standing position, secured by the neck, the hands, and the feet, and that she was kept in it from the moment when she was brought to Rouen until the opening of her trial. However, I never saw her in it. For when I led her out or in she was always unchained.

a prostitute, a sinner, or both; the English and Burgundians, who could not conceive of a young unwed woman traveling with soldiers unless she was sleeping with them, had often called Joan a "whore" because they assumed she *was* one. Certainly, the discovery that she was not a virgin would be a potent weapon to use against her in the trial. In such a case, Cauchon would be able to say not only that she was a sinner but also that she was a liar for having insisted on her virginity. However, the matrons who examined Joan found that she was indeed the virgin she said she was. Neither the fact of her virginity nor the examination itself was ever mentioned in the court records, probably because Cauchon wanted to exclude any information that might portray her in a positive light.

The First Session

Cauchon's biased and unfair treatment of Joan continued at the first session of the initial interrogation process, which was held in Rouen's Bouvreil castle on February 21, 1431. Notaries sitting at tables covered with pens and parchment had the task of recording the official minutes, or records, of the proceedings. As the questioning began, one of these scribes, Guillaume Manchon, immediately noticed that an "unofficial" transcript was also being recorded, which disturbed him greatly. He was also annoyed when Cauchon and his assistants (who did much of the questioning for the bishop) tried to get him to alter the version he himself was recording. Manchon later remembered:

> At the beginning of the trial, during five or six days, while I set down in writing the Maid's answers and excuses [explanations], sometimes the judges tried to constrain me, by translating into Latin, to put into other terms, changing the meaning of the words or, in some other manner, my understanding of what had been said. And [there] were placed two men, at the command of my lord of Beauvais [Cauchon], in a window alcove near to the place where the judges were. And there was a . . . curtain drawn in front of the window so that they should not be seen. These men wrote and reported what was charged against Joan, and suppressed her excuses. . . . And after the session, while collating what they had written, the two others reported in another manner and did not put down Joan's excuses.

The fair-minded Manchon dutifully complained about these deceptive practices, but to no avail, for as he recalled, "On this subject my lord of Beauvais was greatly enraged against me."

Much of this first session was taken up by an argument between Joan and Cauchon over whether or not she should swear to an oath promising to tell the truth about everything that was asked of her. The shrewd young woman apparently did not want to trap herself into having to reveal certain kinds of personal, privileged information, especially about her voices.

CAUCHON: Swear to speak the truth with your hand on the holy gospels in all matters on which you will be questioned.

JOAN: I do not know on what you will question me. It may happen that you will ask me a thing which I shall not tell you.

CAUCHON: You will swear to speak the truth on what will be asked you concerning matters of faith and what you will know [what is within your knowledge].

JOAN: Of my father, of my mother, of all that I have done since I arrived in France [that is, since leaving Domrémy], I will willingly swear; but the revelations made to me by God, I have not told nor revealed to anybody excepting only to Charles, my King, and I shall not reveal them though it cost me my head. I have had that [been told] by my visions and by my secret counsel, to reveal them to nobody. In the next eight days I shall know well whether I am to reveal them.

This painting of Joan at her trial emphasizes her defiant attitude toward Cauchon and her other accusers.

When Cauchon continued to press her to swear an oath, she finally agreed to do so on matters of the faith, but added that she would not divulge certain private information about her revelations.

Joan's Impudence

Joan's refusal to swear the oath Cauchon had wanted her to was only one of many instances in which she showed him and his supporters defiance, stubbornness, and even contempt. That she was so insolent, strong willed, and unafraid irked them, and they grasped at every opportunity they could to get back at her. One blatant example of their cruelty occurred the next day. As a group of churchmen led Joan toward the courtroom for the second session, they passed the castle chapel. She expressed her wish to stop and pray a moment, and the court usher, Jean Massieu, who saw nothing wrong in the request, obliged her. On hearing of this, Cauchon's assistant, promoter Jean d'Estivet, sternly reprimanded Massieu, who remembered the episode this way:

> I took Joan from the prison to the place of jurisdiction and passing in front of the castle chapel; at Joan's request I allowed her, in passing, to make her orison [prayer]. For this I was reproved by [d'Estivet], promoter of the case, who said to me: "Truant, who makes you so bold to allow that excommunicated whore to approach the church without permission? I will have you put in a tower so that you can see neither sun nor moon for a month if you do so again." And when the said promoter perceived that I obeyed him not, he several times placed himself before the chapel door [to bar Joan's entrance].

Joan's impudent attitude was only part of what bothered Cauchon and his assistants. They were genuinely surprised and also quite frustrated that a young peasant girl with no formal education was so consistently able to speak clearly and cleverly, to remember large amounts of complicated material almost word for word, to see through and thwart their attempts to confuse and trap her, and in general to match them intellectually. According to Massieu's testimony:

> When Joan was interrogated there were six assessors with the judges, who put questions to her. And sometimes just when one of them was asking a question or she was replying to it, another would interrupt her; so much so that several times she said to her interrogators: "My dear lords, please take your turns!" I well remember that they often asked Joan questions in several parts, and several of them asked her difficult questions at the same time. Then, before she could reply to one, another

put another question. . . . I was surprised to see how well she could reply to the subtle and tricky questions that were asked her, questions that an educated man would have found it difficult to answer well. The examination generally went on from eight to eleven hours.

Jean Fabri agreed, saying, "Sometimes those who questioned her cut into each other's questions to such an extent that she could hardly answer them. The wisest man in the world would have answered with difficulty." And Pierre Daron, an assistant to the sheriff of Rouen, added the following about her extraordinary powers of memory:

I heard it said by several that during that trial Joan did wonders in her answers and that she had an admirable memory, for once when she was being questioned in a matter about which she had already been questioned a week before, she answered: "I was already asked that on such a day" or "A week ago I was questioned about that and I answered in such-and-such [a] way," although Boisguillaume, one of the notaries, told her that she had not answered, some of those present said that Joan was speaking the truth. The answer for that day was read and it was found that Joan was right. She rejoiced greatly at it, saying [in jest] to this Boisguillaume that if he made a mistake again, she would pull his ears.

Perhaps the most memorable instance of Joan's surprising the court with her ability to think quickly and speak well occurred on the third day of the initial interrogations—Saturday, February 24, 1431. When Cauchon's assistant Beaupère attempted to trap her by asking, "Are you in God's grace?"—to which an answer of yes would have made her guilty of the sin of pride and an answer of no would have been an admission that God had rejected her—she stunned everyone present with the cleverness of her answer. "If I am not," she declared, "may God bring me to it; if I am, may God keep me in it." Having masterfully answered the question while managing to avoid the trap, she added, "I should be the most grieved woman in all the world if I knew myself to be not in the grace of God, and were I in a state of sin, I think that the voice [of God] would not come to me, and I would that all could hear it as well as I."

Was Saint Michael Naked?

As the grueling interrogations continued day after day, the questioners often came back to and harped on topics already covered. For example, they frequently expressed their displeasure with Joan's wearing men's clothes and tried to get her to change into a dress. But she obstinately refused to do so. The following exchange was typical.

BEAUPÈRE: Will you wear women's clothes?

JOAN: Give me some and I will go [leave prison a free woman]. Otherwise I will not accept them. I am satisfied with what I have on since it pleases God that I wear it.

It is unclear why these men were so preoccupied with Joan's attire. By contrast, the scholars who had examined her early in 1429 at

Another of the many later depictions of Joan at her trial captures her questioners' frustration at her continued refusal to do their bidding.

Poitiers at the request of the dauphin had deliberated about the matter, and their conclusion was that since Joan would be leading and living with soldiers, her wearing of male clothes was understandable. Perhaps the churchmen at the trial considered her constant refusal to change her attire a symbol of her resistance to them and hoped her acceptance of women's clothes would be a major step in breaking down that resistance. The interrogators also pressed Joan repeatedly about her voices and revelations, often asking about the appearance and mannerisms of the saints that she claimed paid her visits. From the session of March 1:

QUESTIONER: What figures do you see?

JOAN: I see their faces.

QUESTIONER: These saints which appear to you, have they hair?

JOAN: It's good to know [a snide remark equivalent to "wouldn't you just like to know!"].

QUESTIONER: How do they speak?

JOAN: This voice is beautiful, sweet and humble and it speaks the French language.

QUESTIONER: Does not Saint Margaret speak the English tongue?

JOAN: How should she speak English since she is not on the side of the English? . . .

QUESTIONER: Of what form was Saint Michael when he appeared to you?

JOAN: I saw no crown on him; and of his clothes I know nothing.

QUESTIONER: Was he naked?

JOAN: Do you think that God cannot afford to clothe him?

QUESTIONER: Had he hair?

JOAN: Why should it have been cut off?

From the session of March 3:

> QUESTIONER: Did Michael have wings? And what of the bodies and limbs of Saint Catherine and Saint Margaret?

> JOAN: I have told you everything I know and will not answer you further. . . . I would rather you cut my throat than tell you more.

> QUESTIONER: Did Saint Michael and Saint Gabriel have natural heads?

> JOAN: Yes, so I saw them. And I believe that it was they, as certainly as I believe that God exists.

> QUESTIONER: Do you believe that God made them with heads as you saw them?

> JOAN: I saw them with my own eyes. I will not say anything else.

Cauchon and the Dissidents

After the March 3 session, the sixth held so far, a frustrated and embarrassed Cauchon temporarily adjourned the court. He had invited several prominent Burgundians and Englishmen to watch a "beautiful trial" in which, he bragged, he would easily browbeat and discredit this illiterate peasant girl. Yet after six days of questioning he had failed to break her spirit, and her eloquence and quick wit had matched and even surpassed his own. Deciding that he must alter his strategy, he met every day for a week with his assistants and finally concluded that henceforth Joan would be questioned privately in her prison cell; furthermore, only a few selected assessors would be allowed to watch. As noted medieval historian Frances Gies comments,

> The explanation given publicly for limiting the attendance was that the "various occupations" of the assessors made it difficult for them to be present. The real reason was evidently that Cauchon wished to eliminate assessors sympathetic to Joan and at the same time to make the trial less public.

Bishop Cauchon, accompanied by a scribe, questions Joan in her prison cell. His efforts to break her spirit continued, to no avail, for many weeks.

In fact, there *were* a few assessors and other Burgundian churchmen and laymen who were either sympathetic to Joan or else too honest and upstanding to go along with Cauchon's cruel, shady, and often illegal tactics. In addition to Manchon and Massieu, whose attempts to treat her fairly had greatly angered Cauchon, a small number of widely respected scholars either refused to serve as assessors or openly criticized his handling of the case. For their courageous stands, most received insults, threats, or other abuse. One of these dissidents was Jean Lohier, a distinguished cleric who arrived in Rouen during the lull between Joan's sixth and seventh interrogations and whose support Cauchon was eager to get. As Manchon later recalled:

> When the trial was started, master Jean Lohier, a learned Norman clerk, came to . . . Rouen and there was communicated to him by the Bishop of Beauvais, what was in writing [the records of the first six sessions]. Lohier asked for a delay of two or three days to consider it. He was told that he must give his opinion at once. . . . And master Jean Lohier, when he had read the proceedings, said that it was worthless for several reasons; for as much as it had not the form of an ordinary trial. It was carried on in a place closed and locked where those present were not at liberty to say their full and pure will; they were dealing in this matter with the . . . King of France whose cause Joan supported, without calling himself or anyone from [associated with] him. . . . This woman, who was a simple girl, had no counsel to answer so many

doctors and masters and on great matters, especially those touching upon her revelations. . . . And for all that, it seemed to him [Lohier] that the proceedings were not valid.

Enraged by Lohier's honest critique, Cauchon flew into a rage. The bishop would likely have tried to punish Lohier in some way had the cleric, likely sensing trouble was afoot, not left immediately for Rome. Venting his anger on some of his own supporters, Cauchon bellowed:

> Here is Lohier who wants to wreck our trial with his . . . judgments! He would slander the whole thing and says it is worthless. If he is to be believed, everything is to be done over again, and what we have [already] done is good for nothing. . . . By St. John, we shall do nothing of the sort and will continue our trial as it began!

The Earthly Church Versus the Heavenly Church

And, indeed, Cauchon and his supporters did just that. They resumed Joan's interrogations on March 10, 1431, and held nine

CAUCHON'S REVENGE

Like Jean Lohier, Nicolas Houppeville, a master of theology at the University of Paris, dared to defy Pierre Cauchon. In this later recollection by Houppeville (quoted from *The Retrial of Joan of Arc*), he tells how, after he had refused Cauchon's demand that he serve as an assessor at the trial, the bishop exacted revenge.

> I was sent for one day at the beginning of the trial and I did not go because I was prevented by another case. When I went, on the second day, I was not received; I was, indeed, ordered out of court by the lord Bishop of Beauvais, and that was because I had said earlier, when I was discussing it with Master Colles, that there was a danger in bringing this case for several reasons. This remark was reported to the bishop. That was why the bishop had me put into the royal prisons at Rouen from which I was delivered at the prayer of the then lord abbot of Fécamp. I heard it said that, on the advice of certain people whom the bishop had called together for that purpose, it was decided to send me into exile in England or elsewhere, out of the city of Rouen, which would have been done but for the intervention of the abbot and some of my friends.

more sessions, sometimes scheduling two per day, with the last one taking place on March 17. Perhaps the most important line of questioning that occurred in these sessions concerned the difference between the "Church Militant" and the "Church Triumphant." The medieval Church held that the Church Militant was the holy Church as it existed on earth, with its pope, cardinals, bishops, other clergy, and all good Christians struggling to defeat Christ's enemies; while the Church Triumphant was the heavenly Church, consisting of God, the saints and angels, and the souls of good people who had been saved. Cauchon insisted that Joan stop falling back on her allegiance to her alleged voices and submit to the will of the Church Militant, that is, her present judges. But once more, she remained obstinate.

> QUESTIONER: If it happens that you have done anything which is against the faith, will you abide by the determination of our Holy Mother Church in whom you should trust?
>
> JOAN: Let my answers be seen and examined by clergy and let me be told thereafter if there be in them anything against the Christian faith. . . . If there be anything bad against the Christian faith which God ordains, I would not maintain it and I should be right eager to come to the contrary opinion.
>
> QUESTIONER: The distinction between the Church Triumphant and Militant . . . has been explained to you. I now ask you to submit yourself to the determination of the Church upon what you have done and said of good, as of evil.
>
> JOAN: I will make you no other answer for the present.

Thus ended the first stage of the trial. Cauchon and his assistants now retired to study the testimony and from it to draw up the Articles of the indictment against Joan. As she would soon learn, there would be many charges and they would be exceedingly damning.

Chapter 4

Joan the Defiant

O N March 18, 1431, the day after the last session of Joan's interrogations, Pierre Cauchon, bishop of Beauvais, met with a group of his assistants and some of the assessors who had witnessed the opening phase of the trial. It was decided that Jean d'Estivet would draw up the charges. Following the usual procedure of ecclesiastical courts, these would be in the form of Articles of indictment. About a week later, at a second meeting, the men examined and approved d'Estivet's completed Articles, of which there were seventy; they planned to read these aloud to Joan in court one by one, giving her the opportunity to respond to each. In trials run by the Inquisition, once the formal charges were leveled, the suspect became the accused and was presumed guilty, no matter how much he or she protested innocence. The primary purpose of the second stage of the trial was to give Joan a chance to save her soul by admitting her guilt and begging forgiveness from her judges and from God. This process, which proved grueling and controversial, ended up lasting over two months, in large part because, despite the onset of illness and the continued intimidation of her accusers, Joan remained ever defiant.

Joan Formally Charged with Wrongdoing

The court resumed open sessions on Monday, March 26, in the same chamber off the castle's main hall where the first six interrogations had taken place. Some forty assessors were present, along with the usual groups of notaries. The reading of the Articles and Joan's responses to them took a full two days and covered the same topics brought up in the interrogations, except that this time the straightforward information Joan had earlier given had been interwoven into the text of a series of damning accusations. For instance, under interrogation she had said that her parents had dutifully had her baptized and had brought her up in the Christian faith; the court now put a different spin on this testimony, charging that she had *not* been raised a Christian, but instead had been taught "sorcery, divination [the art of telling the future], and other superstitious practices or magic arts."

Similarly, she had earlier testified that she had heard voices and that these had belonged to saints and angels. Now it was charged that she was "presumptuous" for believing that she, an uneducated girl, could tell a spirit voice from a human voice. And, further, if she did actually hear voices, why had she not readily divulged in full the contents of the conversations she had had with them to these learned and holy men? The fact that she had refused to do so was clear proof that she was hiding something, namely that said voices belonged to evil spirits. Joan of course insisted that she had been telling the truth, that her voices were actually divine and good.

After all the charges had been read and recorded and Joan had duly denied them, Cauchon demanded that she admit her guilt and submit to the Church. She asked for a recess in which to think it over, and on March 31 Cauchon and his assistants again demanded her submission, this time in a session held in her cell.

QUESTIONER: Will you confide yourself to the judgment of the Church which is on earth [i.e., the Church Militant] in all that you have said and done both good and evil, and especially in the cases, crimes, and misdemeanors of which you are accused and in all touching your trial?

JOAN: On that which is asked of me, I will abide by the Church Militant provided it does not command anything impossible to do, and what I call impossible is that I should revoke the deeds I have done and said and what

I have declared concerning the visions and apparitions sent to me by God; I shall not revoke them for anything whatsoever; that which Our Lord has made me do and commanded and will command, I shall not fail to do for any man alive, and in the case of the Church willing me to do otherwise and contrary to the commandment which has been given me by God, I shall not do it for anything whatsoever.

QUESTIONER: If the Church Militant tells you that your revelations are illusions or things diabolical, will you abide by the Church?

JOAN: In that I will always abide by God whose commandment I have always done. . . . And in the case of the Church Militant commanding me to do the contrary, I should not abide by any man in the world but only by our Sire [God] whose good commandment I have always done.

Standing between two guards (at left), Joan confronts Cauchon and the assessors. To save time and effort, they decided to reduce the number of charges against her from seventy to twelve.

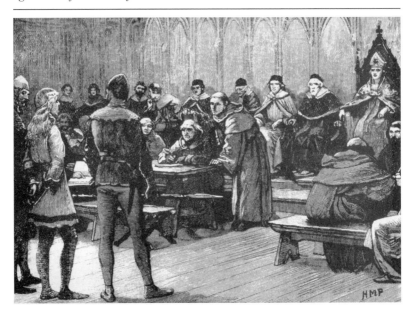

By this response, Joan, still resolute in the sincere belief that all of her testimony was the truth, served notice on her accusers that their list of so-called charges would not intimidate her into submission.

A Streamlined Indictment

Cauchon and his supporters now realized that getting Joan to submit might conceivably take a long time, perhaps weeks or even months. They might have to go over the Articles with her again and again, hammering away at each point until they might finally break her will and force her to admit her guilt. The sheer number of Articles would make their job all the more complex and laborious, so it made sense to streamline the indictment. Guillaume Manchon later recalled:

> It was decided by the councilors and especially by those who had come from Paris, that . . . out of all these Articles and responses there should be made a few short Articles and that the principal points should be summarized to present the matter briefly in order that the deliberations could be better done and more rapidly. It was for that reason that the twelve Articles were drawn up, but it was not I who did them and I do not know who composed or extracted them.

These twelve Articles, distilled from the original seventy, became the official charges leveled against Joan during the rest of her trial. All deliberations and decisions concerning the case, including her sentencing, were based on these charges alone, even though some of them distorted or actually contradicted words or meanings of the testimony from the interrogatory stage of the trial.

The first Article concerned Joan's supposed revelations of angels and saints and stated that the court found these "all false, seductive, pernicious [destructive], that such revelations and apparitions are superstitions and proceed from evil and diabolical spirits." The second, third, and fourth Articles also dealt with Joan's alleged divine visitations, including some she claimed took place in the presence of the dauphin and the archbishop of Reims, as well as her professed ability, thanks to her voices, to foretell future events. The court found these claims "not probable, but rather a presumptuous, misleading and pernicious lie, an undertaking contrary and derogatory to the dignity of angels," as well as "vain boasting."

Article Five concerned Joan's insistence on wearing men's clothing, a serious charge considering her judges' apparent preoccupation with and opposition to her doing so throughout the early stages of the trial. The Article, as later slightly amended by members of the University of Paris, stated:

> You have said that you wore and still wear man's dress at God's command and to His good pleasure, for you had instruction from God to wear this dress, and so you have put on a short tunic, jerkin, and hose with many points. You even wear your hair cut short above the ears, without keeping about you anything to denote your sex, save what nature has given you. And often you have in this apparel received the Sacrament of the Eucharist [Holy Communion]. And although you have been many times admonished to put it off, you would not, saying that you would rather die than put off this dress, unless it were God's command; and that if you were still in this dress and with those of your own party, it would be for the great welfare of France. You say also that nothing could persuade you to take an oath not to wear this dress and bear these arms; and for all this you plead divine command. Regarding such matters, the clergy declare that you blaspheme against God, despising Him and His sacraments, that you transgress divine law, Holy Scripture and the canons of the Church, that you think evil and err from the faith, that you are full of vain boasting, that you are given to idolatry [the worship of idols] and worship yourself and your clothes, according to the customs of the heathen [non-Christian].

The other charges were as follows: Article Six accused Joan of boasting she would kill all those who disagreed with or

Joan wearing her armor. Among the charges against her was her insistence on maintaining male attire.

disobeyed her and called her a "traitor . . . desiring human bloodshed"; the seventh Article chastised her for leaving her parents' house "against their will" (an obvious distortion of "without their knowledge," as had actually occurred) to visit Robert de Baudricourt; the eighth Article declared that she had offended God and the very saints she claimed to hear by attempting to commit the "cowardly" act of suicide while in captivity (she did in fact leap from a sixty-foot tower into a dry moat; however, she had earlier insisted that this was part of an escape attempt); Articles Nine, Ten, and Eleven covered various other claims she had made about her relationships with Saints Catherine, Margaret, and Michael, and accused her of invoking demons, committing blasphemy, and erring from the Christian faith; and finally, the twelfth Article denounced her for refusing to submit to the authority of the Church Militant.

Joan Falls Ill

Before confronting Joan with these charges, Cauchon first sought to legitimize his handling of the case by submitting them to a group of outside assessors, who were asked to render their opinions in writing. He no doubt expected an automatic rubber stamp of approval from these men. Instead, while many of them found the indictment largely sound, some felt that Joan should be given the benefit of the doubt and that the case should be taken to the pope in Rome; and a few even suggested that the Maid might not be guilty of the offenses listed.

Joan Charged with Invoking Demons

From the court memorandum listing the twelve Articles of Joan's indictment (later slightly amended by the University of Paris), this is charge number eleven, dealing with the nature of the apparitions she claimed had paid her visits (quoted from W. P. Barrett's translation of *The Trial of Jeanne d'Arc*).

> You declared that to those whom you call St. Michael, St. Catherine and St. Margaret, you did reverence, bending the knee, taking off your cap, kissing the ground on which they trod, vowing to them your virginity: that you believed in the instruction of these saints, whom you invoked, kissed and embraced, as soon as they appeared to you, without seeking counsel from your priest or from any other ecclesiastic. And, notwithstanding, you believe these voices came from God as firmly as you believe in the Christian religion and the Passion of Our Lord Jesus Christ. Moreover, you said that if any evil spirit should appear to you in the form of St. Michael you would know such a spirit and distinguish him from the saint. And again you said, that of your own accord, you have sworn not to reveal the sign you gave to your king [some secret information, still unknown, shared by her and the dauphin at Chinon]. And finally you added: "Save at God's command." Now touching these matters, the clergy affirm that if you had the revelations and saw the apparitions of which you boast in such a manner as you say, then you are an idolatress, an invoker of demons, an apostate from the faith, a maker of rash statements, a swearer of an unlawful oath.

Infuriated by these dissenting opinions, Cauchon ignored them and prepared to proceed with the next phase of the trial, known as the "charitable admonitions," a regular feature of Inquisition courts. Once the accused was formally charged, thereby establishing guilt, he or she was administered a combination of questioning and counseling aimed at producing a full admission of that guilt. If deemed necessary, torture could also be used. Though seen as inhumane today, at the time such physical coercion was thought to be justified on the grounds that it helped to discover the truth and subsequently to save the accused person's soul.

But shortly before the admonitions were to begin, Joan fell ill in the prison. The nature of her illness remains unknown;

however, a physician who examined her, one Jean Tiphaine, later testified:

> When Joan was ill the judges sent me to visit her and I was taken to her by the man d'Estivet. In the presence of d'Estivet, of Master Guillaume de la Chambre, Master of Medicine, and of several others, I felt her pulse to learn the cause of her sickness and I asked her what was the matter and where she felt pain. She answered me that a carp [a freshwater fish] had been sent to her by the Bishop of Beauvais, that she had eaten of it, and that that was the cause of her sickness. Then d'Estivet scolded her saying that that was false and he called her wanton [immoral], saying, "It is you, wanton, who has eaten shad [another variety of fish] and other things which have done you harm." She answered that she had not and many insulting words were exchanged between Joan and d'Estivet. Later, wishing to know more of Joan's sickness, I heard it said by people who were there that she had vomited many times.

Per the common medical custom of the time, the doctors bled Joan, opening a vein in her arm and allowing a certain amount of blood to flow out into a pan. In this way, they believed, some or all of the "impurities" that were in her blood and had caused her sickness would drain away.

With little regard to Joan's health, Cauchon decided to go ahead with the admonitions while she was still ill (he may actually have been trying to take advantage of her weakened condition, the easier to get her to submit). The following is a part of the exchange that took place between Cauchon and Joan in her cell on April 18, 1431:

> JOAN: It seems to me, in view of the sickness that I have, that I am in great danger of death; and if it be so that God would do his will upon me, I ask to have confession and the sacrament of the Eucharist and to be buried in holy ground.

JOAN EXAMINED BY DOCTORS

When Joan fell ill in mid-April 1431, a group of doctors attended her in her prison cell. Among them was Guillaume de la Chambre, who later recorded this recollection (quoted from *The Retrial of Joan of Arc*).

> In what concerns her sickness, the cardinal of England and the Earl of Warwick [captain of Rouen's Bouvreuil castle, where Joan was held] sent for me. I presented myself before them with Master Guillaume Desjardins . . . and other physicians. The Earl of Warwick told us that Joan has been taken ill, as had been reported to him, and that he had sent for us that we might take care of her, for not for anything in the world would the [English] King have her die a natural death. The King, indeed . . . would not have her die excepting at the hands of justice, and that she be burnt. . . . We palpated her [touched her body to aid in diagnosis] on the right side and found her feverish. We therefore decided to bleed her. When we made our report to the Earl of Warwick, he said: "Be careful when bleeding her, for she is cunning and might kill herself." Nevertheless, she was bled, which gave her immediate relief. As soon as she was thus better, came one master Jean d'Estivet who exchanged insulting words with Joan and called her "whore, wanton." She was by this so upset that she became feverish again and fell ill again. That came to the earl's knowledge, who forbade d'Estivet to insult Joan thenceforth.

CAUCHON: If you [are to] have the sacraments of the Church you must [first] declare yourself a good Catholic and submit to the Church.

JOAN: I am not able to say anything else to you at present.

CAUCHON: The more you fear for your life because of the sickness which you have, the more should you amend your ways. . . .

JOAN: If my body dies in prison, I expect you to put it in holy ground, and if you do not have it put there, I put my trust in God [to do so]. . . .

CAUCHON: Since you ask that the Church give you the sacrament of the Eucharist, will you submit yourself to the Church Militant? . . .

JOAN: God I love, I serve Him and am a good Christian and I would help and sustain the Church with all my power.

This shows that even in her weakened state, Joan was well able to handle herself and remained unintimidated, even in the face of Cauchon's suggestions that she might not end up with a proper burial, a dreadful and alarming prospect to the medieval mind.

The Threat of Torture

The second session of admonitions took place on May 2 in the room off the great hall. Joan had recovered from her bout of illness, and her defiant expression signaled that she was ready once more to do battle with her accusers. Again the questioners called on her to submit to the Church Militant; and she repeatedly fell back on her love for God, who, she said, had motivated all of her deeds. They asked her if she felt obliged to obey any earthly judge, to which she responded, "I have a good master, that is, God, whom I trust in everything, and not anyone else." At this, they reminded her that if she did not believe in the earthly Church, she must be a heretic and an unrepentant heretic would surely be burned alive. This cruel threat did not seem to frighten her. Even if she saw the flames before her, she answered, she would still maintain the truth of the testimony she had given thus far.

The questioners then launched into another tirade about her male attire. They demanded that she change into a dress and she offered to do so, providing they allowed her to wear it to church, take Communion, and afterward change back into what she was wearing. They took this answer as another example of her insolence (which to some degree it was) and told her that it was blasphemy to claim that God and the saints had made her wear male clothes; to which she replied categorically that she had never committed any sort of blasphemy.

Exchanges like these, with Joan steadfastly maintaining her defiant stance, continued. Realizing that they were getting nowhere, her accusers decided to threaten her with torture; they knew that most people being tried by the Inquisition were so terrified of torture that the mere sight of the various common torture instruments made them submit. So on May 9 Cauchon, accompanied by some assessors and also Rouen's official executioner, took Joan to the donjon, or central tower stronghold, of the castle. They showed her the hideous implements of pain and again put their questions to her, the implication being that if she did not submit they would use these implements on her. The executioner later remembered:

> I saw her at Rouen castle when me and my companion [the assistant executioner] were sent for to put Joan to the torture. She was then questioned for some time and she answered with much prudence, so much so that those who were there marveled.

Still unintimidated, Joan concluded her remarks by declaring resolutely, "Truly, though you were to have my limbs torn off and send the soul out of my body, I should not say otherwise;

Joan, still wearing men's tights and doublet, stands before Cauchon in this nineteenth-century painting of the trial.

Officials of the notorious Inquisition torture prisoners in an attempt to obtain confessions. Note the crucifix and open Bible at right, signs of the Church's sanctioning of such practices.

and if I did tell you otherwise, I should always thereafter say that you had made me speak so by force." Deciding that, at least for the moment, torture would be of no avail, the churchmen postponed it. The executioner recalled, "Finally we withdrew, I and my companion, without having laid hands on her person."

"Obey the Church and Submit"

It must have seemed to Cauchon and his supporters that they were running out of options. Perhaps Joan might give in if they showed her that it was not only they, whom she obviously despised, who realized the depth and seriousness of her guilt, but also all other learned men and institutions. On May 14 Cauchon submitted the twelve Articles against her directly to the prestigious scholars of the University of Paris, asking for their official judgment. Five days later he and the court assessors met privately to hear this judgment read. The university declared that Joan's statements about her visions were lies; that her revelations and voices were spirits sent by Satan; that she had committed blasphemy by saying that God or his saints had inspired her to wear male clothing; that her leap from the tower was indeed suicidal and, therefore, a sin; that she had erred from Christian teachings and principles; and that she was a liar, a sorceress, and a vain boaster.

On May 23, armed with this new ammunition, Joan's accusers admonished her again in her cell. This time Pierre Maurice, a churchman of Rouen cathedral, was with them. He informed her of the university's damning opinion of her and then, evidently in a friendly, pleading tone designed to win her over, said the following:

> Joan, dearest friend, it is now time, near the end of your trial, to think well over all that has been said. Although you have four times already . . . been most diligently admonished for the honor and reverence of God, for the faith and the law of Jesus Christ . . . although you have been shown the perils to which you expose your body and soul if you do not reform yourself and your sayings and correct them by submitting your acts and your words to the Church . . . up till now you have not wished to listen. . . . When the lord judges received the deliberations of the University they decided that you should to this end be once more admonished, warned of your errors, scandals and other crimes, and that we should beg, exhort and advise you by the bowels of Our Lord Jesus Christ . . . to correct your words and submit to the judgment of the Church, as every loyal Christian is bound and obliged to do. Do not permit yourself to be separated from Our Lord Jesus Christ who created you. . . . Obey the Church and submit to its judgment; know that if you do not, if you persevere in this error, your soul will be condemned to eternal punishment and perpetual torture. . . . Let not human pride and empty shame, which perhaps constrain you, hold you back because you fear that if you do as I advise you will lose the great honors which you have known. For the honor of God and the salvation of your body and soul must

come first: You will lose all if you do not [do] as I say, for you will separate yourself from the Church and from the faith you swore in the holy sacrament of baptism. . . . Therefore, in view of all these things, on behalf of your judges . . . I admonish, beg and exhort you . . . correct and amend these errors, return to the way of truth, by obedience to the Church and submission in all things to her judgment and decision. By doing so you will save your soul and redeem, as I hope, your body from death; But if you do not . . . know that your soul will be overwhelmed in damnation and I fear the destruction of your body. From these ills may Our Lord preserve you!

To this admonition, the still defiant Joan replied:

The way that I have always spoken and held to in this trial, that will I still maintain. And if I was brought to judgment and saw the fire lit and the faggots [bundles of kindling] ready, and the executioner ready to stoke the fire and that I be within the fire, yet should I not say otherwise and should maintain what I have said in the trial even unto death.

With these words, Joan finally convinced her judges that any further admonitions would be a waste of time. They therefore declared the trial officially at an end and announced that the next day they would deliver the sentence of the court. After she had courageously endured the court's almost relentless onslaught of questions, harassment, and threats for over three months, Joan realized that her day of judgment was finally at hand.

Chapter 5

Joan the Condemned

THE LAST SEVEN DAYS of Joan of Arc's life began on May 24, 1431. In the morning churchmen and guards led her from her cell and took her to the cemetery of Rouen's Abbey of St. Ouen, there to hear her sentence pronounced. When she arrived, she saw that two platforms had been erected, one for her judges, the notaries, and other officials to stand on and the other for her. Three documents had been prepared for the occasion. One was an abjuration, a renunciation of her former statements and claims, in essence an admission of guilt; apparently, the Inquisition officials hoped that at the last minute Joan might finally give in and submit to their authority. The other two documents consisted of alternate sentences—one to be pronounced if she did in fact abjure, the other if she did not.

The Maid might have died that very morning had she not agreed to sign the abjuration, which she did. However, the circumstances surrounding this agreement, and indeed the entire ceremony in the cemetery, remain controversial; it is highly probable that Joan did not understand what she was agreeing to by signing the document. In any case, thanks to the zeal of those who desired her death and also to her own stubbornness, her abjuration, valid or not, did nothing more than buy her a few extra days of life.

Abjuration

The ceremony in the cemetery attracted a large crowd of spectators, including a number of English soldiers. On one of the platforms gathered several notables, including a cardinal, a bishop, a representative of the English king, and the principal assessors from the trial. Joan was to share her platform with Guillaume Erard, a University of Paris master who had come to preach her a public sermon before the reading of her sentence. Jean Massieu, the court usher who had frequently escorted her from place to place during the trial, was also to stand with her. Shortly before Joan ascended the platform, one of the assessors from the trial, Nicolas Loiseleur, took her aside and, according to Guillaume Manchon's later testimony, told her:

> Joan, trust me and you will be saved. Accept your [women's] dress, and do everything they tell you, or you are in danger of death. And if you do as I say, you will be saved, and will have great benefit, and no harm, but will be turned over to the Church.

Then Massieu helped her to climb the platform steps. Erard began his sermon, in which he solemnly explained that all Catholics should obey the Church. Joan, he said, had separated herself from the "unity of our Holy Mother Church" by her many serious errors and crimes. At one point, according to witnesses, he sharply denounced Charles VII as a heretic and Joan boldly interrupted him. "By my faith, sir," she told him, "with all respect, I say and swear to you, on pain of my life, that he is the most noble Christian of all." Surprised by this interruption, Erard ordered Massieu to "make her be quiet."

Exactly what happened in the next few moments is somewhat uncertain, for the many witnesses stood in different places, some near to Joan and others more distant, and their recollections vary. Evidently, on finishing his sermon, Erard asked Joan if she would consider revoking her former heretical deeds and words—that is, would she agree to abjure? To this, she replied, "I refer myself to God and our holy father the Pope," which was essentially an appeal to have the pope hear her case. Erard explained that this was not possible because the pope was too far away, and he called on her to submit instead to her local judges, which was the accepted procedure.

Erard repeated this call for submission three times. When Joan remained silent, Cauchon began to read the sentence that would have condemned her, given her up to English custody, and consigned her to the flames. As the bishop spoke, Massieu, Loiseleur, and Erard each urged her to relent and sign the abjuration; and she suddenly indicated that she would consider it. Hearing this, Cauchon stopped reading the sentence and a few moments later someone brought the abjuration document.

Suspicion and Controversy

Two aspects of Joan's signing of this document remain suspicious and controversial. First, did she understand fully what she was signing and what would happen after she did so? The recollections of several of the witnesses present suggest that she did not. For instance, after expressing her interest in abjuring she turned to Massieu, told him she did not know what abjuration was, and begged him to explain. Also, it is likely that she believed, as Loiseleur had told her earlier, that in exchange she would be granted her life, suffer no harm, and be handed over to the Church. In a church prison she would be guarded by nuns rather than by English soldiers and in general receive far better treatment than she had in Bouvreuil castle. Joan apparently also believed that once in church hands she would be allowed to receive Holy Communion on a regular basis. She did not seem to grasp that her abjuration amounted to a full admission of guilt and that her captors could thereafter do whatever they pleased with her. Massieu remembered:

> When Joan was required to sign this document there was great murmuring among those who were present. . . . I warned Joan of the danger which threatened her in the matter of signing this abjuration document. I saw well that Joan understood neither the document nor the danger.

Nevertheless, the Maid affixed her mark to the paper, the authenticity of which constitutes the second controversial aspect of the episode. The document that entered the court record was a long tract in which the signer admitted she was a miserable sinner and a blasphemer, that her saints were evil spirits, and so on. But a later investigation showed clearly that this was not the document Joan had signed on the platform that day. According to Massieu:

> The schedule [abjuration document] was handed to me to read to her, and I read it to her. I well remember that in the schedule it was written that she must never carry arms again, or wear men's clothing, or cut her hair short, also a number of other things which I do not remember. And I am certain that this schedule was eight lines long and no more, and I am positive that it was not the one quoted in the report of the case. The one I read was different than the one set out in the report, and it is the former one that Joan signed.

A STATE OF INVINCIBLE IGNORANCE

In this excerpt from the lengthy preface to his great play *Saint Joan*, British playwright George Bernard Shaw comments on Joan's pure and simplistic view of the Christian faith, which, he contends, made it difficult for her to comprehend the formal doctrines and procedures the churchmen were using to condemn her.

> The tragic part of the trial was that Joan, like most prisoners tried for anything but the simplest breaches of the ten commandments, did not understand what they were accusing her of. . . . Her attachment to the Church was very different from the Bishop's [Cauchon's], and does not, in fact, bear close examination from his point of view. She delighted in the solaces the Church offers to sensitive souls: to her confession and communion were luxuries beside which the vulgar pleasures of the senses were trash. Her prayers were wonderful conversations with her three saints. Her piety seemed superhuman to the formally dutiful people whose religion was only a task for them. But when the Church was not offering her her favorite luxuries, but calling on her to accept its interpretation of God's will, and to sacrifice her own, she flatly refused. . . . The enormity of Joan's pretension was proved by her own unconsciousness of it, which we call her innocence, and her friends called her simplicity. . . . She was in a state of invincible ignorance as to the Church's view; and the Church could not tolerate her pretensions without . . . waiving its authority. . . . Thus an irresistible force met an immovable obstacle, and developed the heat that consumed poor Joan.

This drawing, published in Harper's Magazine *in 1896, depicts Joan signing the document of abjuration.*

Thus, it appears that Cauchon and his assistants had tricked Joan into giving them what they wanted—a full confession.

The English Robbed of Their Prize?

Immediately after Joan signed the abjuration, Cauchon read the alternate sentence: life imprisonment. And then he delivered Joan a much harsher blow. When she remarked, "Come now, among you men of the Church, take me to your prisons and let me no longer be in the hands of these English," the bishop gruffly ordered the guards, "Take her to where you found her." Contrary to what Joan expected would happen if she signed the paper, she was to remain in the custody of those who, in their hatred of her, would surely continue to chain her, torment her, and deny her the solace of taking Holy Communion. This, suggests noted scholar Régine Pernoud,

was Joan's real sentence of condemnation. For there is a fact which dominates the whole trial, the fact that Joan was detained in a lay prison and guarded by English warders, while being tried for heresy: now she should have been held in an ecclesiastical prison . . . where she would have been guarded by women. This is the fundamental contradiction which makes it impossible to see this trial as a normal trial for heresy—although Cauchon insisted that it was so—and which underlines, quite clearly, its political character. Joan was a political prisoner whose enemies contrived to get her dealt with as a heretic in order to destroy the prestige which her personal saintliness and her extraordinary exploits had made for her.

Cauchon was no doubt satisfied with himself, having won what he believed was a righteous victory over an enemy of the Church. But the English did not share his elation. They had been eagerly looking forward to taking charge of Joan and burning her, when quite unexpectedly the man they considered one of their staunchest Burgundian allies had seemingly robbed them of their prize. Jean Fave, an eyewitness to the events immediately following the scene in the cemetery, later stated:

> The leading Englishmen were very angry with the Bishop of Beauvais, the doctors, and other assessors at the trial, because she had not been convicted, and condemned and delivered over to execution. . . . Some of the English, in their indignation, raised their swords to strike the bishop and the doctors on their way back from the castle—but they did not strike them—saying that the King had ill spent his money on them.

Joan languishes in her prison cell during her last few days of life. Having signed the abjuration, she mistakenly assumed that she would be transferred to a Church prison.

But whatever people may have thought at the time, Joan's reprieve from the executioner turned out to be only temporary. Once back in her cell, she was supplied with a dress, which she put on, and her hair was shaved off as a sign of her penitence. However, only three days later, the news spread through Rouen that Joan had once more defiantly donned her male attire. Though it is difficult to tell precisely what occurred in those fateful few days, it appears that she may have been badgered into doing so by persons who hoped to lead her into a relapse, that is, a rejection of her abjuration and return to her former defiant stance. At the time, a relapsed heretic was seen as a loathsome creature who was both beyond and unworthy of help. If the Inquisition ruled that Joan had relapsed, it would surely turn her over to the English for execution.

A number of different witnesses later offered accounts, some of them contradictory, of how Joan resumed wearing men's clothes. According to Massieu, the day after she had put on the dress, her English guards stripped it off her and flung a bundle of male clothing at her; she protested but they left her no other choice but to remain naked, so she finally put on the clothes. Another witness claimed that "a great English lord" entered her cell one night and tried to rape her, after which she switched back to men's attire to discourage any further such attacks. Others, including Manchon, supported this version, saying that Joan tearfully complained to them that the English had "had much wrong and violence done to her in prison when she was dressed in women's clothes."

Relapse

Whatever Joan's reasons for changing her clothes, during these same days she also underwent a change in attitude. Cauchon, another judge, and eight court assessors entered her cell on May 28, 1431, to find her as stubborn and defiant as she had been throughout the trial. Perhaps not realizing the full import of her words, she now proceeded to damn herself beyond all rehabilitation. She claimed that she would keep her men's attire because the churchmen had not kept their promises to unchain her and allow her to attend Mass and Holy Communion. And she readily admitted that the voices of her saints had returned to counsel her.

CAUCHON: Have you not made abjuration and promised especially not to resume man's clothes?

JOAN: I would rather die than remain in irons; but if it be permitted me to go to mass and I be taken out of irons and that I be put in a pleasant prison, and that I have women [as guards], I will be good and do what the Church wishes.

CAUCHON: Since that Thursday [the day she signed the abjuration], have you heard the voices of Saints Catherine and Margaret?

JOAN: Yes. . . . God has sent to me by Saints Catherine and Margaret great pity for the mighty betrayal to which I consented in making abjuration . . . to save my life, and that I was damning myself to save my life. . . . All that I said and revoked that Thursday, I did only because of fear of the fire. . . . I have never done anything against God and against the faith . . . and for what was contained in the . . . abjuration, I did not understand it. . . . If the judges wish it I will resume women's clothes; for the rest, I will do nothing about it.

Cauchon must have been overjoyed. By damning herself as a relapsed heretic, Joan had given him a simple and perfectly legal way to satisfy both the Inquisition and the English who had been hounding him since the abjuration. According to a witness, on encountering a group of English nobles and soldiers in the castle courtyard after leaving Joan's cell that day, he chortled to them, "We've got her!"

Death in the Marketplace

The next day the death cart arrived at the castle. Massieu and one of the court assessors, Martin Ladvenu, both of them weeping openly, placed Joan in the cart. Nicolas Loiseleur, also overcome with emotion, tried to climb onto the vehicle to beg her

As Joan marches to her death, guards restrain priest Nicolas Loiseleur, who rushes forward and begs forgiveness from the condemned maid.

forgiveness, but the earl of Warwick restrained him for fear the English guards might kill him. The cart, flanked by nearly a hundred armed English soldiers to discourage any would-be rescue attempts, now moved through the streets to Rouen's marketplace, the Vieux Marché. There, a tall scaffold had been erected; on it stood a wooden stake, to which the prisoner would be tied, surrounded by bundles of wood ready to be kindled. Attached to the bottom of the platform was a sign reading: "Jeanne, called the Virgin, liar, pernicious, seducer of the people, diviner, superstitious, blasphemer of God, braggart, idolater, invoker of devils, apostate, and heretic."

After Joan had been removed from the cart, the huge crowd that had gathered in the marketplace heard another of the court assessors, Nicolas Midi, deliver a sermon. This concluded, Cauchon stepped forward to pronounce the sentence. He briefly listed her crimes and explained how the Church had tried diligently to help Joan see the error of her ways. "Nonetheless," he

FEARS THAT THEY HAD BURNED A SAINT

Years after Joan was executed, Isambart de la Pierre, an assessor at her trial, gave this testimony about the day of her death (quoted from *The Retrial of Joan of Arc*).

One of the English, a soldier who particularly loathed Joan and who had sworn to carry a faggot [bundle of twigs] to her pyre with his own hand, was struck with a stupor or a kind of ecstasy when he was doing so and heard her crying on the name of Jesus in her last moments. He was taken to a tavern near the Vieux Marché to be restored to his senses with the aid of strong drink. And when he had eaten with a friar of the Dominican order, this Englishman confessed to the friar, who was an

This engraving, bearing the title "The Maid of Orléans," includes a halo over Joan's head, foreshadowing her later sainthood.

Englishman, that he had committed a grievous sin, and that he repented of what he had done against Joan, whom he considered a saint. For it seemed to this Englishman that he had seen a white dove flying from the direction of France at the moment when she was giving up the ghost. And the executioner . . . that same day, came to the Dominican convent and said to me that he greatly feared he was damned, for he had burned a saint.

told her crudely, "time and time again you have relapsed, like a dog that returns to its vomit." Then he excommunicated her, officially separating her from the body of the Church "as an infected limb," and handed her over to the secular authorities.

Wasting little time, the executioner took her to the scaffold. Massieu, who had come to feel both respect and affection for her, was allowed to remain with her almost to the end, and he later recalled:

> She asked most fervently to be given a cross. And when an Englishman who was present heard this he made her a little one out of wood from the end of a stick, and handed it to her. She received it and kissed it most devotedly. . . . And while she was saying her prayers and piously lamenting I was urgently pressed by the English, and by one of their captains in particular. . . . While I was doing my best to comfort her on the scaffold, this man said to me, "What, priest, are you going to keep us here till dinnertime?" Then without any formality or any reading of the sentence, they dispatched her straight to the fire, saying to the executioner: "Do your duty." And so while she was still uttering devoted praise . . . to God and the Saints, she was led off and tied to the stake. And her last word, as she died, was a loud cry of "Jesus."

Afterward, guards carefully gathered the young girl's ashes and threw them into the Seine River so that no one could later

---

A GREAT WEEPING

The scribe Guillaume Manchon left this moving recollection of Joan's last moments and his own subsequent grief and regret (quoted from *The Retrial of Joan of Arc*).

> I saw Joan led to the scaffold. There were seven or eight hundred soldiers around her, carrying sticks and swords; so many indeed that there was no one bold enough to speak to her except Friar Ladvenu and Master Jean Massieu. She listened patiently right through the sermon, and afterward uttered her plea for God's grace, her prayers, and her lamentations, with such remarkable devotion that the judges, prelates, and all those present were moved to great weeping and tears when they saw her utter her pitiable griefs and sad plaints. I never wept as much for anything that befell me, and could not finally stop weeping for a whole month afterward. With a part of the money which I was paid for the case, I bought a little missal [prayer book], which I still possess, to remind me to pray for her. I never saw such signs of penitence at any Christian's end.

As the flames begin to consume her death pyre, Joan clutches the cross hastily made for her by a sympathetic Englishman in the crowd of onlookers.

claim she had escaped; except, that is, for her heart. Shaking in superstitious fear, the executioner later swore that no matter what means he used—oil, sulfur, or charcoal—Joan's heart would not burn.

Epilogue

Joan the Martyr

J OAN OF ARC'S ASHES may have disappeared into the Seine, but
her memory lives on, ironically greatly eclipsing those of her
detractors, judges, and even the king she fought to enthrone.
"Her life was the shortest," comments one of her modern biogra-
phers, "her active career the briefest and most striking in its
achievement, while her fame remains the greatest and most endur-
ing of any woman signalized in secular history." In death, Joan
became a martyr to the cause of the French nationalists she had
championed and also to the struggles of many other oppressed
groups and unjustly accused individuals over the centuries. And

*This later depiction of Joan's last moments is titled "The Sheriff Reading the
Death Sentence of Joan of Arc."*

her story has inspired generations of writers and artists. Scholar Charles Lightbody sums it up this way:

> After a lapse of more than five centuries, every detail of her life, her visions and her achievement remains significant to countless numbers of [people], alike in her own country and in many other parts of the globe. This peasant girl who never got out of her teens, who had an active career of little more than two years, whose life ended in heroic martyrdom at an age when girls today leave school—this peasant girl left such an impress upon the history of her time that many members of each succeeding generation of Western civilized men have thought it worthwhile to record, often in full length, their varied comments upon her, in countless histories and biographies, dramas, poems, pictures, [and] works of music.

Joan's Immediate Legacy

Because Joan's rise to prominence was so meteoric, with her capture, trial, and death so quickly following, in the wake of her passing the events of her exploits, trial, and martyrdom blurred together to form a single legacy. The immediate impact of that legacy was the victory of French nationalism over the English occupation forces, a process that had already been set in motion by Joan's rallying of the Armagnacs and getting Charles to Reims to be crowned. Despite his weak rule as a young man, inspired by Joan's legacy Charles went on to become an effective, powerful leader; and slowly but relentlessly, from the disunity and turmoil of the Hundred Years' War, he forged a new nation—a unified France that has endured to the present.

Directly following Joan's death, Charles's forces continued the offensive she had begun and wrested more towns from enemy control. This pressure forced the Burgundians to the bargaining table, and in 1435 the Armagnacs and Burgundians concluded the Treaty of Arras, permanently depriving the English of the ally they needed to make further conquests in France possible. Forced into a slow but inevitable retreat, the English soon

⚖ ARTILLERY REPLACES FEUDAL KNIGHTS

Joan's exploits and martyrdom coincided with profound social, political, and military changes that were then reshaping medieval society. In this excerpt from her book *Joan of Arc: The Legend and the Reality*, noted historian Frances Gies explains how these changes affected the conclusion of the Hundred Years' War.

The transition from feudal to monarchic power was evident most significantly in the military field. Joan's epic is filled with evidence of the rise of the new money-based royal military power amid the disappearance of the old anarchic [disunited] feudal fighting class. As the army became professionalized, knights disappeared not so much out of it as into it, blending with plebeian [common] "men-at-arms" who wore the same armor, rode the same horses, and received (by 1440) the same pay. Great nobles—dukes, counts, earls—continued to maintain their own military forces, but though they could hire captains, archers, and men-at-arms, the new artillery arm was beyond any but a king's means. Thus the artillery, whose military value Joan had appreciated, became, because of its cost, an element of significance in the social-political evolution. The pioneering artillery force of Charles VII was strengthened and improved . . . until it became an effective arm in the field as well as in siege operations. When the Hundred Years' War entered its final phase in 1449, it took on for the first time the character of a French invasion of English territory. The walled towns and castles of Normandy fell with astonishing rapidity . . . and the English field army was destroyed at the battle of Formigny (April 15, 1450).

had to abandon Paris. And by 1449 they had been confined to the regions of Normandy in the north and Gascony-Guienne in the southwest. The following year Charles delivered them a stunning defeat at Formigny in Normandy; and in 1453 he decisively defeated them again at Castillon in the south, finally succeeding in driving them completely from French soil in fulfillment of Joan's promise that he would do so.

During his final thrusts against the enemy, Charles liberated Rouen in 1449 and there found the records of Joan's trial. He appointed one of his councilors, Guillaume Bouillé, to study these records, an inquiry that soon blossomed into a full-scale investigation and retrial aimed at clearing and rehabilitating

Joan. Over the course of the next seven years, hundreds of witnesses were located and questioned. Cauchon and some of the others involved in the first trial were now dead; but many others who had known Joan were still living, among them Moreau, d'Aulon, Manchon, Massieu, de Chambre, and Ladvenu, all of whom provided valuable testimony about her life and death. On July 7, 1456, in the cathedral of Rouen, the Trial of Rehabilitation rendered its final verdict, which said in part:

> We say, pronounce, decree, and declare the said trial and sentence [of condemnation by the Inquisition] to be contaminated with fraud, calumny, wickedness, contradictions, and manifest errors of fact and law, and together with the abjuration, the execution, and all their consequences, to have been and to be null, without value or effect, and to be quashed. . . . We proclaim that Joan . . . did not contract any taint of infamy and that she shall be and is washed clean of such.

Poetic Justice

Joan's rehabilitation was the first step in the building of her legend as a heroic and saintly character. But though her name had been cleared among her countrymen, her former enemies, the English, took longer to come around. English chronicles of the 1400s and 1500s typically distorted the facts of her exploits and depicted her as a liar, a witch, a prostitute, a deranged fanatic, and so on. These works culminated in the famous *Chronicles*, published in 1587 by Raphael Holinshed, which in turn became the main source Shakespeare used in writing his historical play *Henry VI, Part 1*. Shakespeare has Joan capture and burn Rouen (which of course she did not), cruelly taunt the dying English regent, the duke of Bedford (he actually died four years after she did), and, when sentenced to die, foully call a curse of death, mischief, and despair upon the English (also a fabrication). The play, though undoubtedly great literature, goes out of its way to paint an inaccurate and unfair picture of Joan.

In time, however, people everywhere, including the English, came to see Joan as a hero, due in large degree to a modern resurgence of interest in her legacy that began in the nineteenth century. In 1841 French historian Jules Michelet published his huge *History of France*, and the three chapters he devoted to Joan became so popular that they were republished in a separate volume. Even more decisive in igniting worldwide interest in her story was French scholar Jules Quicherat's *The Processes of Condemnation and Rehabilitation of Jeanne d'Arc, Called the Virgin*, published between 1841 and 1849. This massive five-volume work was the first to include the complete texts of both trials, along with all chronicles, public documents, and letters about Joan. And it inspired hundreds of histories, poems, plays, and novels in the century that followed. Perhaps the most famous of these was British playwright George Bernard Shaw's brilliant 1923 play, *Saint Joan*, which is still often performed.

Shaw's use of "Saint" in the play's title was not an expression of his personal whimsy, but a reference to Joan's canonization, which had taken place three years before. Completing an initiative begun by Pope Leo XIII in the 1890s, in 1920 the Catholic Church officially made Joan a saint. This came far too late to help Joan, of course; but it did offer a kind of closure to and healing of a long-standing wound the Church had opened in condemning and executing her. The Church's gesture also stands as an expression of poetic justice for one of history's most memorable figures: In life she was an illiterate peasant girl who claimed to hear the voices of saints; in death, she became one of their number.

Timeline

1339   England's King Edward III invades France, initiating the so-called Hundred Years' War.

1411   John the Fearless, leader of the French Burgundians, seizes control of Paris, igniting civil war in France.

1412   Jeanne d'Arc, known to history as Joan of Arc, is born in the town of Domrémy, in northeastern France.

1415   England's King Henry V invades France and defeats the French at Agincourt, south of Calais.

1425   At the age of thirteen, Joan first claims to hear the voices of angels and Christian saints, who have given her the mission of aiding Charles VII, the dauphin, the rightful heir to the French throne.

1429   Joan meets the dauphin and convinces him of her sincerity; riding at the head of his army, she is instrumental in stopping the Burgundian siege of the city of Orléans.

1430   Joan is captured by the Burgundians and handed over to their allies, the English.

1431   From February 21 to March 17 Joan undergoes interrogations by church officials in the first phase of her trial for heresy; on May 24, under duress, Joan signs an abjuration, admitting her guilt; on May 28, she relapses, rejecting the abjuration; on May 29 the Church hands her over to the English, who burn her at the stake in the marketplace at Rouen.

1453   Continuing the initiative Joan had begun, Charles drives the English from France.

1456   After a retrial, in which the case against Joan is thoroughly reviewed, her name is cleared.

1920   The Catholic Church declares Joan a saint.

For Further Reading

Jean Anouilh, *The Lark.* Adapted by Lillian Hellman. New York: Random House, 1956. This is the excellent play about Joan's trial by the great French dramatist Anouilh (1910–1987), whose other often-performed plays include *Antigone* (1944) and *Becket* (1959). The original production of *The Lark* opened on Broadway in November 1955, with Julie Harris as Joan, Christopher Plummer as Warwick, and Boris Karloff as Cauchon.

Tracey Christopher, *Joan of Arc: Soldier Saint.* New York: Chelsea House, 1993. A brief but well-written overview of the main events of Joan's life, including her military exploits, capture, trial, and martyrdom.

Frances Gies and Joseph Gies, *Life in a Medieval Village.* New York: HarperCollins, 1990. This entertaining and informative work by two of the most respected modern medieval historians examines the major aspects of the medieval peasant society in which Joan of Arc grew up, including its religion, justice system, kinds of work, and family and social customs. Somewhat advanced for young people but well worth the effort. Note that Frances Gies's book about Joan of Arc (see Works Consulted) is one of the best of its kind; and also look for the other excellent books about the medieval period by Frances and Joseph Gies, including *Life in a Medieval City* and *Women in the Middle Ages.*

André Maurois, *An Illustrated History of France.* Translated by Henry L. Binsse and Gerard Hopkins. New York: Viking Press, 1960. A handsomely mounted book with numerous dramatic photos and reproductions of old paintings and engravings. The easy-to-read text gives a straightforward overview of the main events of French history, including Joan's victories at Orléans and Patay and other exploits.

Maurice Boutet de Monvel, *Joan of Arc.* New York: Viking Press, 1980. This is a fine modern reprint of de Monvel's 1896 volume,

Jeanne d'Arc, one of the most famous children's books ever published. The author produced his own magnificent color drawings, several of them accurate and dramatic depictions of medieval warfare, which are here beautifully reproduced.

Brian Williams, *Joan of Arc*. New York: Marshall Cavendish, 1989. Part of the publisher's Children of History series, this is a general overview of Joan's life written for basic readers.

Author's Note: Several films have been made about Joan of Arc, most of them European. Of those in English and available on videotape, look for: *Joan of Arc* (1948), directed by Victor Flemming, starring Ingrid Bergman and José Ferrer, based on Maxwell Anderson's play *Joan of Lorraine;* and *Saint Joan* (1957), directed by Otto Preminger, starring Jean Seberg and Richard Widmark, based on George Bernard Shaw's play of the same name.

Works Consulted

Christopher Allmand, *The Hundred Years War: England and France at War, 1300–c. 1450.* New York: Cambridge University Press, 1988.

W. P. Barrett, *The Trial of Jeanne d'Arc: Translated into English from the Original Latin and French Documents.* London: Routledge, 1931.

John Bourchier (Lord Berners), trans., *The Chronicles of Froissart.* London: Macmillan, 1899.

Winston S. Churchill, *The Birth of Britain.* New York: Bantam Books, 1956.

Robert Cole, *A Traveler's History of France.* New York: Interlink, 1995.

Marshall B. Davidson, *The Horizon Concise History of France.* New York: American Heritage, 1971.

Frances Gies, *Joan of Arc: The Legend and the Reality.* New York: Harper and Row, 1981.

George Holmes, ed., *Oxford History of Medieval Europe.* Oxford: Oxford University Press, 1988.

Wilfred T. Jewkes and Jerome B. Landfield, eds., *Joan of Arc: Fact, Legend, and Literature.* New York: Harcourt, Brace and World, 1964.

Archer Jones, *The Art of War in the Western World.* New York: Oxford University Press, 1987.

Charles W. Lightbody, *The Judgements of Joan.* Cambridge, MA: Cambridge University Press, 1961.

Régine Pernoud, *Joan of Arc by Herself and Her Witnesses.* Translated by Edward Hyams. New York: Stein and Day, 1966.

91

————, *The Retrial of Joan of Arc: The Evidence at the Trial for Her Rehabilitation.* Translated by J. M. Cohen. New York: Harcourt, Brace and World, 1955.

Edward Peters, *Inquisition.* Berkeley: University of California Press, 1988.

Vita Sackville-West, *Saint Joan of Arc.* 1936. Reprint, New York: Doubleday, 1991.

W. S. Scott, ed. and trans., *The Trial of Joan of Arc: Being the verbatim report of the proceedings from the Orleans Manuscript.* Westport, CT: Associated Booksellers, 1956.

George Bernard Shaw, *Saint Joan.* Baltimore: Penguin Books, 1952.

Clara Winston and Richard Winston, *Daily Life in the Middle Ages.* New York: American Heritage, 1975.

Index

Agincourt, Battle of, 17
Armagnacs
  conflict with Burgundians, 16, 18
armor, medieval, 40
Arras, Treaty of, 84
assessors, 43
Aulon, Jean d', 28, 41
  on Joan at court in Chinon, 25

Baudricourt, Robert de, 22
Beaupère, Jean, 9
Bouillé, Guillaume, 85
Bouvreuil castle, 7, 46
Burgundy/Burgundians, 9
  agree to truce, 38
  alliance with England, 15, 18
  capture of Joan at Compiègne,
    41, 42
  conflict with Armagnacs, 15
  defense of Paris by, 39–40

Cagny, Perceval de, 39
Catholic Church
  canonization of Joan by, 87
  Church Militant vs.Church
    Triumphant, 56
Cauchon, Pierre, 8, 44
  submits Articles for judgment,
    68
Chambre, Guillaume de la, 65
Charles VII (dauphin, king of
  France), 8, 14
  coronation at Reims, 37
  is disinherited, 18
  meets Joan, 22, 24–25
Charles VI (king of France)

agrees to Treaty of Troyes, 18
  death of, 19
Chronicles (Holinshed), 86
Chronicles of Froissart, The , 13
Compiègne
  capture of Joan at, 41
Crécy, Battle of, 12, 13

dauphin. *See* Charles VII

Edward III (king of England), 11
England/English
  alliance with Burgundians and,
    15, 18
  basis of claim to French throne,
    16
  defeat of
    at Formigny, 85
    at Orléans, 35
    at Patay, 37–38
  fear of Joan by, 42
  invasion of France by, 11, 16
Erard, Guillaume, 72
Estelin, Beatrice d'
  on Joan's childhood, 16
Estivet, Jean d', 49, 57

Fabri, Jean, 45, 50
Fastolf, John, 19, 37
Fave, Jean, 76
Formigny
  English defeat at, 85
France
  civil war in, 17
  invasion of, 11, 16
Froissart, Jean, 13

93

Gies, Frances, 11, 53, 85

Henry V (king of England)
death of, 19
launches invasion of France, 16
Henry VI, Part 1 (Shakespeare),
86
History of France (Michelet), 87
Holinshed, Raphael, 86
Houppeville, Nicolas, 55
Hundred Years' War, 7
beginning of, 11–12
military changes affecting
outcome of, 85

Inquisition, 43
Articles of, 44
reading of, 57–69
presumption of guilt under, 57

Jean, duke of Alençon, 35
Joan of Arc
as defiant under threat of
torture, 67–68
canonization of, 87
childhood of, 14
ennobling of, 41
entry into Reims, 37
execution of, 81–82
illness of, 63–64
journey of, 20–22
leads French army, 25–26
legacy of, 84–86
Loire campaign and, 35–36
meets Charles VI, 24–25
meets the dauphin, 22
mission of, 20, 27
signing of abjuration by, 71
controversy over, 72–75

trial of
Church Militant vs. Church
Triumphant and, 56
first stage of, 44
questioning at, 50–54, 66
reading of Articles, 57–60
swearing of oath, 47–48
Trial of Rehabilitation of, 86
virginity of, 45–46
voices heard by, 20
wounding of, 33–34
John of Luxembourg, 41, 42
John the Fearless, 18
Journal of the Siege of Orléans, 30

Laxart, Durand, 21
Leo XIII (pope), 87
Lohier, Jean, 54
Loire campaign, 35–36
Loiseleur, Nicolas, 72, 78
longbows, superiority of
at Battle of Agincourt, 17
at Battle of Crécy, 13

magic arts, 58
Manchon, Guillaume, 72
on Joan's last moments, 81
on transcription of trial, 47
Massieu, Jean, 49, 77
on abjuration document, 74
on Joan's treatment in prison,
46
Maurice, Pierre, 69
medieval towns, defenses of, 29
Michelet, Jules, 87
Middle Ages
military changes during, 85
town defenses in, 29
Mide, Nicolas, 79

Moreau, Jean, 45
Musnier, Simonin, 15

Orléans
  entry of Joan into, 28, 30
  siege of, 27
  victory of French at, 9, 30–35

Paris, 38
  French fail to take, 39
Patay
  French victory at, 9, 37, 38
Pierre, Isambart de la, 80
*Process of Condemnation and
  Rehabilitation of Jeanne d'Arc,
  Called the Virgin, The*
  (Quicherat), 87

Quicherat, Jules, 87

Reims, 27
  entry of Joan into, 37
Rouen
  liberation of, 85

Saarbruck, Robert de, 20
Shakespeare, William, 86
Shaw, George Bernard, 74, 87
St. Crispin's Day, 17
St. Joan (Shaw), 74, 87

Tourelles (fortress)
  French attack on, 32–35
towns, medieval, 29
Troyes, Treaty of, 18

Vaucouleurs (fortress), 21

witchcraft, 28

Picture Credits

About the Author

Historian and award-winning author Don Nardo has published over eighty books. In addition to this volume on Joan of Arc, his other studies of historical figures include *The Trial of Socrates; Franklin D. Roosevelt: U.S. President;* and biographies of Julius Caesar, Cleopatra, Thomas Jefferson, Charles Darwin, and John Wayne. Mr. Nardo, who also writes screenplays and composes music, lives with his wife, Christine, on Cape Cod, Massachusetts.